HELMUT GNEUSS

English Language Scholarship:
A Survey and Bibliography from the
Beginnings to the End of the
Nineteenth Century

Medieval & Renaissance Texts & Studies

Volume 125

HELMUT GNEUSS

English Language Scholarship:
A Survey and Bibliography from the
Beginnings to the End of the
Nineteenth Century

MEDIEVAL & RENAISSANCE TEXTS & STUDIES
Binghamton, New York
1996

Library of Congress Cataloging-in-Publication Data

Gneuss, Helmut.
  English language scholarship: a survey and bibliography from the
beginnings to the end of the nineteenth century / Helmut Gneuss.
    p.   cm. — (Medieval & Renaissance Texts & Studies ; v. 125)
    Includes bibliographical references and index.
    ISBN 0–86698–130–6
    1. English philology—Study and teaching—History. 2. English philol-
ogy—Study and teaching—Bibliography. I. Title. II. Series.
PE65.G58 1995
420.7—dc20   94–45610
                                                                  CIP

This book is made to last.
It is set in Bembo,
smythe-sewn and printed on acid-free paper
to library specifications

Printed in the United States of America

Contents

Preface

This outline of the history of English language studies is an expanded version of a paper first read in February 1989 at a session of the Philoso-phisch-Historische Klasse of the Bayerische Akademie der Wissenschaften. It was published in 1990 in German, in the *Sitzungsberichte* of the Bavarian Academy, together with a bibliography. In this English version a number of changes have been made in text and footnotes, the bibliography has been brought up to date, and an index to the bibliography has been added.

I wish to thank all who helped me at various stages of the work: Angelika Schröcker for putting Part I on to computer; Gabriele Knappe, M.A., for computerizing both versions of the bibliography and for pains-takingly verifying every item listed; Dr. Michael Korhammer for solving all the computer problems; Dr. Lucia Kornexl and Ursula Lenker, M.A., for compiling the index to the bibliography and other help. Lucia Kornexl, in particular, has been a most unselfish, meticulously critical reader of the whole. Mr. Mark Atherton provided a draft translation of Part I into English, which here appears in a revised form. I am grateful to Professors Mario Di Cesare and Paul Szarmach for including *English Language Scholar-ship* in the Medieval & Renaissance Texts & Studies series.

H. G.

HELMUT GNEUSS

English Language Scholarship:
A Survey and Bibliography from the
Beginnings to the End of the
Nineteenth Century

PART I: THE STUDY OF ENGLISH

Introduction

During the past few decades, in the wake of new developments in research and teaching, we have seen a veritable flood of publications in linguistics. In view of this fact, and in view of the importance attached to
theories and methods in many of these books and articles, it was inevitable
that linguists should turn their attention to the history of the discipline, and
it is pleasing to note how interest in this area has grown in recent years, as
can be seen from numerous publications in the field, from meetings like the
International Conferences on the History of the Language Sciences since
1978, and from the formation of scholarly associations, such as the Henry
Sweet Society founded at Oxford in 1984.[1]

If we recall, moreover, that the history of linguistics is not a completely
new discipline (the first studies of the history of English grammar and
lexicography, for instance, were published around the middle of the last
century), it seems strange that the scholarly study of English—the language
most widely investigated and used in linguistics—has not so far received a
comprehensive survey of its history. There is indeed a wide-ranging
literature on individual topics, areas and periods, but we find this work
treating primarily the developments in English grammar and lexicography
from the sixteenth century to the end of the eighteenth. The nineteenth
century has received less attention, and until very recently the Middle Ages
were a largely unexplored territory. [1–6]

A full survey of the history of English linguistics (or rather: the history
of the science of the English language, for this is what I am concerned
with here) cannot, of course, be achieved within the narrow limits of a
revised and expanded version of a lecture. In what follows here, I will
confine myself to an attempt to sketch the outlines on which a compre-

---

[1] Cf. sections 1–4a of the bibliography in Part II below. All further references to the
sections of the bibliography will be given in square brackets.

hensive treatment could be based. My emphasis will be on the tasks, methods and aims of linguistic scholarship in the past, rather than on ideas and theories; I will also consider the successes and failures in the synchronic and diachronic description—and in the inventories—of English (which, incidentally, are closely related to the theory and practice of language teaching) and the conditions under which this linguistic work was carried out and published.

I would ask for the reader's indulgence towards the inevitable cuts and simplifications in a brief overview such as this; the inclusion or omission of names and titles does not necessarily imply a value judgment. The many and various developments of the twentieth century, in particular those of the last few decades, will require separate treatment by a competent author. A further limitation of what follows is the state of research in many areas, which does not allow us to form a conclusive picture as yet, and for this reason my study must inevitably be of a preliminary nature. Thus, for the 'Middle English' period, from the twelfth century to the end of the fifteenth century, we need an inventory of the linguistic writings produced or read in England, whether extant in manuscripts or otherwise attestable; and for the nineteenth century, a thorough study and analysis is required of our field, in particular of the grammars, dictionaries and manuals of style then published in enormous numbers.

1. The Anglo-Saxon Period

Interest in the vernacular and a conscious concern with the use and employment of the English language reach far back into the first millennium AD. They must have existed even in the pre-literate period, and there is evidence to support such an assumption: we need only think of the adaptation of the runic alphabet to the phonology of early English, of the role of vowel quantity in Germanic and Anglo-Saxon meter, or of the language of poetry in general. Books and writing reached the Anglo-Saxons in the seventh century, but the number of people capable of reading and writing was limited, and remained so for centuries. It is of course this minority that we are dealing with in our discussion of the knowledge of languages and the study of language in Anglo-Saxon England. [7]

All such study in Anglo-Saxon times was primarily devoted to Latin. But there can be no doubt that the late Roman system of grammar with its categories and its specific terminology was also applied to the English language. To gain a clear view of the situation, we need to distinguish a three-stage process of development within the period of about four centuries with which we are concerned here:[2]

The first stage covers the time from the conversion to Christianity to about the beginning of the ninth century (naturally we cannot assign exact dates to these periods). It is marked by the flowering of Anglo-Saxon culture, especially in Northumbria and Southern England; its key figures are Theodore of Tarsus, Aldhelm, Bede, and Alcuin.

The second stage falls roughly within the confines of the ninth century. It must be seen as a period of general decline and decay of learning—actually before the onset of the Viking invasions and settlement in the latter half of the century, which led to the destruction of many libraries and the loss of most of the books imported into England or written there during the first period.

The third stage, from the end of the ninth century to the late eleventh century, is characterized by the reforming zeal of King Alfred and, in particular, the Benedictine bishops of the tenth century (Dunstan, Æthelwold and Oswald). Supported above all by the new or refounded monasteries in Southern England and the Midlands, their efforts led to the development of a cultural setting founded on religious learning, the study of language and literature, and extensive book-production; in this setting, the English language had an extremely important role to play.

Grammars of Latin and English

Already in the first period, scholars in Anglo-Saxon England had access to most of the important grammatical writings on the Latin language that had been transmitted from late Roman times. This is clear from Alcuin's catalogue of authors in the library of York, and from source studies of the grammatical and metrical works of Anglo-Saxon authors of the early period (Aldhelm, Bede, Tatwine, and Boniface). These writers were able to use the grammars and commentaries of Audax, Charisius, Diomedes, Donatus, Phocas, Priscian, Servius, and Sergius, as well as the encyclopedic works of Martianus Capella, Cassiodorus, and Isidore of Seville, to name only the most important. [8] Latin had to be learned by the Anglo-Saxons as a foreign language, but just for this purpose the works of the Roman

---

[2] On this periodization see Helmut Gneuss, "Anglo-Saxon Libraries from the Conversion to the Benedictine Reform," *Settimane di studio del Centro italiano di studi sull'alto medioevo* XXXII, 1984 (1986), 643–88.

grammarians were not ideally suited as textbooks. The main problem for learners was to acquire a mastery of Latin accidence, and this is clearly taken into account in two grammars, written by Anglo-Saxons at the end of the seventh and the beginning of the eighth centuries, which later became known and used on the Continent; their authors were Tatwine, a priest in Breedon-on-the-Hill in Leicestershire (731–34 Archbishop of Canterbury), and Boniface, the 'Apostle of Germany,' at this time still teaching at the monastery of Nhutscelle (Nursling) in Hampshire.[3] [9]

The extent of the influence of Irish grammarians in early Anglo-Saxon England cannot easily be judged. It seems likely that the Anglo-Saxons knew the curious work by Virgilius Maro Grammaticus. [10] What is certain is that the rich holdings of grammatical writings in English libraries were decimated in the upheavals of the ninth century: in the reform period of the tenth century, Latin and the teaching of Latin again played an important role; yet, if we examine the extant manuscripts and booklists, and the source studies on Ælfric's *Grammar,* they show that in the tenth and eleventh centuries the grammatical writings of only two Roman authors appear to have been generally accessible. As we would expect, these are Donatus and Priscian; to these we should add Book I, on grammar, in Isidore's *Etymologies,* and the anonymous *Excerptiones de Prisciano.* Besides these writings, we have only one manuscript of part of the *Ars de Verbo* of Eutyches and one of the grammar by Phocas, a mention of an *Ars* of Sedulius Scottus (in a booklist of the late eleventh century), and some evidence that Byrhtferth of Ramsey knew the commentary on Donatus by Sergius.

Four of the Anglo-Saxon grammar teachers of the tenth and early eleventh centuries are known to us by name: Æthelwold (from about 954 Abbot of Abingdon, 963–84 Bishop of Winchester), his pupil Ælfric (from 987 teaching at the abbey of Cerne in Dorset and from 1005 Abbot of Eynsham), Abbo of Fleury, who from 985 to 987 served as a teacher (apparently not entirely by choice) at Ramsey Abbey, and Abbo's pupil, Byrhtferth, also active at Ramsey. It can be shown that all of these—with the exception of Abbo, who was not an Anglo-Saxon—were concerned with the use and teaching of the English language. This is hardly surprising, in view of the important role that English had assumed since the time

---

[3] A later source also names Theodore of Tarsus as a teacher of grammar; see Walter Berschin, *Greek Letters and the Latin Middle Ages: From Jerome to Nicholas of Cusa,* rev. ed., trans. J. C. Frakes (Washington, D.C., 1988), 121–25.

of King Alfred, not only in poetry, but also in literary and non-literary prose; from the tenth century onwards there even developed an Old English standard language, used in writing throughout the country. Moreover, our evidence points to a circle of writers trained at, or related to, Æthelwold's school at Winchester, who sought to standardize the use of the vocabulary, but presumably also Old English usage in other areas. Standardization is even found in the handwriting of the period; it is hardly a coincidence that from the second half of the tenth century, Latin and English texts were written in two different types of script (Caroline and Insular minuscule respectively).

The most important linguistic work from this period is Ælfric's *Grammar*. Its main source were the (still unpublished) *Excerptiones de Prisciano*, chiefly based on the works of Priscian and Donatus. In its structure, Ælfric's book is conceived as a grammar of Latin, but it was intended to further the understanding of both languages, as Ælfric himself expressly says in the introduction directed to his young pupils: "quatinus ... in isto libello potestis utramque linguam, videlicet Latinam et Anglicam, vestrae teneritudini inserere. ..." Consequently, all his explanations and definitions are in English or in both languages, and all the Latin examples have also been translated into English. The result is a contrastive grammar, with a heavy emphasis on morphology and especially accidence. Questions of syntax are only occasionally considered, but a well-known attempt has been made to establish a grammatical terminology in English. As far as the teaching of Latin was concerned, Ælfric wished to provide a schoolbook that would bridge the gap between the elementary introduction of Donatus's *Ars minor* and the rather demanding *Institutiones grammaticae* of Priscian. Ælfric was clearly successful in this undertaking. The number of manuscripts of his *Grammar* still extant today leaves no room for doubt that in the eleventh century every library in England owned at least one copy of this textbook that had evidently become indispensable. It was still used in the twelfth century, even by speakers of French. [11]

Synonymy, Rhetoric, Glossography, Translation and Borrowing

Other areas of grammar were also studied from the earliest Anglo-Saxon period, along with the then known linguistic disciplines; no doubt such studies were closely linked to the observation and use of the vernacular. Here, in the area of grammar and in the discipline called *differentiae* belongs

Bede's treatise *De orthographia,* a teaching manual whose title is deceptive, for it deals with questions of Latin orthography, morphology, synonymy [12], syntax, and numerous other problems.[4] Further topics are dealt with in the later *Quaestiones grammaticales* by Abbo of Fleury, who answers the queries of his pupils at Ramsey, especially about quantity, stress, and pronunciation, and who also employs the contrastive method.

That the authors of Old English poetry and prose made use of rhetorical devices has been demonstrated repeatedly. It would seem that the Anglo-Saxons did not have ready access to the full range of classical teaching on rhetoric, and that they may not have known the rhetorical writings of Cicero and Quintilian, or the anonymous *Rhetorica ad Herennium;* these texts are not found in English libraries before the twelfth century. On the other hand, the Anglo-Saxons were well acquainted, from the earliest times, with the system of the tropes and figures, which appeared in grammatical treatises, especially in Part III of the *Ars maior* of Donatus. This was the basis for Bede's *De schematibus et tropis,* with examples, however, taken from the Bible, and for Byrhtferth's treatment of the same topic, based on Bede, but now in English, in his *Handboc.* [13]

The Anglo-Saxons practised what might be called the comparative lexicology of English and Latin, as can be seen in numerous texts and translations, in interlinear glosses and glossaries. Glossography began as early as the seventh century at the school of Theodore and Hadrian in Canterbury. A collection of glosses from this school has a long and complicated history in the following centuries: it very soon reached the Continent, while in England parts of it found their way in one form or another into glossaries compiled in early and late Anglo-Saxon England. These glossary materials merit our attention for two reasons: they form part of the literary heritage that must have survived the disasters of the ninth century, and

---

[4] On synonyms and *differentia* in the Middle Ages, see below p. 38. Among the linguistic materials preserved from the Anglo-Saxon period are various unstudied grammatical texts, and collections of alphabets, including runic alphabets. For the grammar texts, see Gneuss, "The Study of Language in Anglo-Saxon England," *Bulletin of the John Rylands University Library of Manchester,* 72 (1990): 6 n. 11, and Lapidge in *Wulfstan of Winchester: The Life of St Æthelwold,* ed. Michael Lapidge and Michael Winterbottom (Oxford, 1991), lxxxvi-lxxxvii. The runic alphabets have been thoroughly treated by René Derolez, *Runica Manuscripta: The English Tradition* (Bruges, 1954). A Hebrew alphabet, not previously noticed, occurs on fol. 42 of MS. Cambridge, Corpus Christi College 356.iii (late tenth century; St. Augustine's, Canterbury). The *Versus cuiusdam Scoti de alphabeto* were also known in England; they have been edited by Fr. Glorie, *Variae Collectiones Aenigmatum,* CCSL 133A (1968), 729–40.

they contain—from a very early date—English as well as Latin explanations, and thus constitute the beginnings of bilingual lexicography in England. Among the later glossaries, those of the tenth and eleventh centuries still extant, one already has the format of a small dictionary; compiled around the year 1000, and preserved in London, B. L. MS. Harley 3376, it originally consisted of more than 12,000 entries, of which about a third contained interpretations in English. Besides the collections of glosses which, together with their lemmata, were taken from various Latin texts and later arranged alphabetically, the Anglo-Saxons also knew the 'class-glossary,' a type of collection designed for study and teaching, in which the words are grouped according to subject matter, a good example being the glossary evidently provided by Ælfric to accompany his *Grammar*. [14]

The ways in which the Anglo-Saxons dealt with questions of meaning and word-formation can clearly be seen from the rich translation literature which began in the reign of Alfred. Particularly instructive are also the numerous interlinear versions of Latin texts, and the results of linguistic borrowing, of creating English loan-formations and semantic loans on the model of Latin. The so-called syntactic glosses deserve mention here, too; these fairly frequent devices consist of marks designed to facilitate the understanding of Latin sentence constructions.

It should be borne in mind that Latin (and its late forms as spoken on the Continent) was not the only foreign language with which the Anglo-Saxons came into contact. As is evident from loanwords and other types of borrowing in Old English, there were contacts not only with Celtic (British and Irish) and Norse in Britain itself, but also with Old Saxon and the emerging French language. Greek was mostly conveyed through Latin texts; Greek words occur, for instance, in Isidore's *Etymologies* and in glossaries. It has now been convincingly established, however, that Greek was actively and successfully taught at the school of Theodore and Hadrian, and Bede, too, may well have had knowledge of the language. [15] The Anglo-Saxons and their successors also made use of the etymological method of antiquity, according to which it was sufficient to establish a mere phonetic resemblance between one particular word and another one in order to explain the first; furthermore, words could be given a Christian interpretation through etymology, and this method was also applied to the English language. [16]

2. The Middle English Period

In the 'Middle English' period—the High and late Middle Ages in England—the conditions for the study of English changed. From the late
eleventh century, three main trends are apparent:

1. The role of Latin was considerably strengthened, a development due
   not only to an increase in the standard of learning in churches and
   monastic institutions, but also to a broadening of the educational system to allow for the teaching of the laity.
2. French took its place side by side with English as a written and
   spoken language and even replaced it in certain areas, but from as
   early as the thirteenth century it lost its position as a mother tongue
   and had to be learned by all who wanted to use it. [18]
3. In written usage, the late Old English standard was replaced by the
   English dialects, all of which were once again, and for a considerable
   time, on an equal footing.

Under these conditions there does not appear to have been much reason
or opportunity for the descriptive treatment or study of English. Evidence
from this period, however, bears witness to the fact that even then, in the
twelfth and thirteenth centuries, the interest in the mother tongue continued. Apart from the development of local scribal traditions, an early
attempt at a reform of English spelling deserves special mention. In the late
twelfth century, Orm, an Augustinian canon in South Lincolnshire, wrote
a collection of verse homilies in which he introduced an orthography that
made a not quite consistent distinction between long and short vowels; his
system does not, however, appear to have gained a following. In the first
half of the thirteenth century, an unknown monk at the cathedral priory
of Worcester tried to keep Old English texts understandable for his contemporaries by means of extensive glossing in Anglo-Saxon manuscripts; he
also made a copy of Ælfric's *Grammar*. Earlier, Gerald of Wales (Giraldus
Cambrensis) had shown an interest in linguistic history in his *Itinerarium
Kambriae* and *Descriptio Kambriae* (written in 1191 and 1194 respectively).
In these works he noted the relationship between Greek, Latin, Welsh and
other languages, and in the *Descriptio* (I.6) he gave a competent explanation
of the differences between the English dialects of his time, considering
characteristics of the Northern dialects as an effect of the *irruptiones* of
Danes and Norwegians. [17]

Grammars and Textbooks of Latin;
Speculative Grammar

Throughout the Middle English period, the study of language remained above all the study of the Latin language.[5] Latin grammar set the standards, and it was the only grammar taught until the fourteenth century.[6] Which books and authorities in this field were studied can be gathered from surviving library catalogues, wills, inventories, and manuscripts, although, as I pointed out in the Introduction, we still lack a full survey of works on language that were written or read in England during the period. Here, as on the Continent, we find texts intended for learning Latin at school or for the study of grammar at university: of the late Roman grammarians, (apart from a few manuscripts of Eutyches and Phocas) mainly Donatus—particularly his *Ars minor* and, usually in this period, only Book III of his *Ars maior,* the so-called *Barbarismus*—and Priscian; it seems notable that most of the surviving English manuscripts of his *Institutiones grammaticae* were written in the twelfth century.[7] From the thirteenth century onwards, two books are found in nearly every school and library which, despite their pedagogical shortcomings, quickly became standard works and exceeded all other grammatical writings—apart from Donatus and Priscian—in significance, and in the number of copies, in England as well as on the Continent. These were the verse grammars of Alexander de Villa Dei, the *Doctrinale,* and of Evrard de Béthune, the *Graecismus.* In these and other grammatical writings of the period, phonology is treated scantily or not all; by contrast, the parts of speech and accidence ('etymology') are given extensive treatment; syntax is restricted mostly to concord and government, while stress and quantity are usually covered, as well as grammatical faults (barbarisms and solecisms), and the tropes and figures.

Also in general use were aids for teaching and learning Latin, especially its vocabulary, by three English authors: the *Oratio de utensilibus ad domum*

---

[5] In the *Prima Pastorum* of the *Wakefield Plays,* the first shepherd uses *by gramere* (line 387) in the sense of 'in Latin'.

[6] On the knowledge of Greek by such scholars as Robert Grosseteste and Roger Bacon in the thirteenth century, see Berschin, *Greek Letters,* 249–55. A *Donatus graece* is listed in the library catalogue of the cathedral priory of Canterbury, compiled about 1170; see Michael Lapidge in *Anglo-Saxon England,* 4 (1975), 80 n. 1.

[7] Donatus, Priscian, and Phocas are also the grammarians mentioned by Richard of Bury in his *Philobiblon* (chap. ix), completed in 1345. For Priscian's undiminished importance in late medieval England, see Robert E. Kaske, [22.3] p. 41 n. 25.

regendam by Adam de Parvo Ponte (also known as Adam of Balsham; he taught at Paris in the twelfth century); the *De nominibus utensilium* (a vocabulary covering Latin nouns for household utensils and much else) and the *Corrugationes Promethei* (on figures of speech, accents, orthography and difficult biblical words) by Alexander Neckam (1157–1217), and several works by John of Garland (c. 1195–c. 1272 ?), who studied at Oxford and taught at Toulouse and Paris, above all his *Dictionarius* (a handbook for learning Latin vocabulary), the *Distigium* (verses with difficult words; perhaps only ascribed to John ?), the *Synonyma* and *Equivoca;* his *Compendium grammaticae* seems to have been rather less common.[8] [19]

Besides these works that were mainly serving practical needs, a number of linguistic treatises with completely different aims began to appear from the second half of the thirteenth century: the speculative grammars. Having fallen into almost complete oblivion for centuries, they have recently met with a great deal of interest and attention. These books were the first universal grammars in the history of linguistics, based on the conception of a common, universal system underlying all languages. Their authors, the *modistae,* regarded the study of language as a philosophical and logical science; their interest centered not on sounds and pronunciation, but on the meaning and function of the parts of speech—analyzed by means of the *modi significandi*—and on syntactic relations, and it was in the field of syntax that they made lasting contributions to the science of grammar. Speculative grammar was a subject of university studies, which—later rejected by the Humanists—seems to have had little immediate influence on the development of English grammar. Moreover, it would appear that most of the speculative treatises by continental writers of the thirteenth and fourteenth

---

[8] The numerous French and English glosses in the manuscripts of these manuals have now been thoroughly studied, and edited, by Tony Hunt, *Teaching and Learning Latin in Thirteenth-Century England,* 3 vols. (Cambridge, 1991). For the Middle English period, we still lack an inventory of writings on Latin grammar by English authors, starting with the *Metalogicon* (I.xiii–xxv) by John of Salisbury. Richard Hunt and Geoffrey Bursill-Hall have done valuable preparatory work in this area. [17.2; 17.6] The role played by the above-mentioned grammars and manuals, particularly those of John of Garland and Alexander Neckam, is well seen in the will (1358) of William Ravenstone, master at St. Paul's School, London, which includes the grammar by John of Garland and the important commentary on Priscian by Petrus Helias. See Edith Rickert, "Chaucer at School," *Modern Philology* 29 (1931–32): 257–74, and the same author's *Chaucer's World* (New York, 1948), 121–26, and cf. now Patrizia Lendinara, "The *Oratio de utensilibus ad domum regendam pertinentibus* by Adam of Balsham," *Anglo-Norman Studies XV,* ed. Marjorie Chibnall (Woodbridge, 1992), 161–76.

centuries never reached England. However, the grammar by Thomas of Erfurt (ascribed for a long time to Duns Scotus) was certainly known there, and English scholars themselves contributed quite early to the new movement with the *Summa grammatica* of Roger Bacon and with anonymous works ascribed to Robert Kilwardby and Robert Grosseteste. Two works on the *modi significandi,* supposedly written by Albertus Magnus, were printed in England in the late fifteenth century. [20]

Latin Grammar Taught in English

For the development of a grammar of the English language written in English the reform of Latin teaching in the fourteenth century played a decisive part. This reform has to be seen in connection with the changing role of French, now no longer a native language, and also with the increase in educational opportunities for a wider section of the laity.[9] In his translation of Ranulf Higden's *Polychronicon,* John Trevisa, around 1385, relates that from the middle of the fourteenth century the method of teaching Latin had changed. It was about this time that John of Cornwall, an Oxford schoolmaster, began to hold his Latin classes in English (hitherto teaching had been in French), and English examples are in fact included in his (as yet unpublished) *Speculum grammaticale,* written in 1346.[10] He soon found a following, and by the end of the fourteenth century teaching manuals were appearing in which Latin and English were compared, and in which English was even used to explain Latin grammar. These were in particular grammatical works for the beginner, written by or ascribed to John Leland or Leyland, who taught as a schoolmaster at Oxford by about 1400 (he died in 1428); as their various versions reveal, they found a wide dissemination in manuscripts and early printed editions. Only recently have they become accessible in a comprehensive modern edition (by David Thomson), and they show, apart from some shortcomings to be expected at this stage, remarkable insight into the structural differences between

---

[9] An instructive guide to our knowledge of the literacy of the laity in London is Sylvia Thrupp, *The Merchant Class of Medieval London [1300–1500]* (Ann Arbor, 1948), chap. iv.1. For literacy in the early Middle English period, see M. T. Clanchy, *From Memory to Written Record: England 1066–1307,* second ed. (Oxford, 1993).

[10] It cannot, however, be ruled out that English was already used for teaching grammar in the Oxford grammar schools of the thirteenth century; see *Munimenta Academica, or Documents Illustrative of Academical Life and Studies at Oxford,* ed. Henry Anstey, Rolls Series, 50 (London, 1868), II.lxx and 438; see also D. A. Kibbee [18.5], p. 56, n. 25.

Latin and English. They employ a standard terminology in English (*noun,
gender, tense,* etc.) that obviously goes back to the time when lessons were
in French; its general currency may be inferred from occurrences in
English literary texts from the late fourteenth century onwards.[11] The
most important of these grammatical texts are: *Accidence,* a treatment of the
parts of speech and their inflection, indebted to the *Ars minor* of Donatus;
Comparacio, on the forms of gradable adjectives and their syntactic con-
struction; *Informacio,* on syntax, particularly the use of the cases; and
Formula, a further treatise on syntax.[12] [21]

The Beginnings of Lexicography

These grammatical textbooks were supplemented by collections of Latin
sentences with English equivalents (or English sentences followed by Latin
versions) known as *Vulgaria* or *Latinitates,* which served as illustrations to
grammatical rules; the method here employed is also, of course, found in
the grammars themselves. [23] There were, in addition, numerous bilingual
word-lists, entitled *Nominale* or *Verbale,* likewise intended for teaching
purposes and arranged in groups according to subject matter; a full, systematic study of such word-lists is still needed. [24]

This brings us to the beginnings of English lexicography, which from
the fifteenth to the seventeenth centuries was essentially bilingual. The
tradition of Anglo-Saxon glossaries, which usually contained selections of
Latin words—mostly in alphabetic order—with Latin and/or English interpretations, had come to an end in the twelfth century. They were followed
and replaced by glossaries devoted to special subjects and, above all, by the
new monolingual works that sought to cover and explain etymologically
the full lexis of the Latin language: the *Elementarium* of Papias (completed

---

[11] Early evidence for the new grammatical terminology is to be found in *Piers Plowman*
C.iv.335–410; Prologue to the Wycliffe Bible, chap. 15, ed. with notes by Anne Hudson,
Selections from English Wycliffite Writings (Cambridge, 1978), 67–72, especially p. 68; *On the
Properties of Things: John Trevisa's Translation of Bartholomaeus Anglicus, De Proprietatibus
Rerum,* ed. M. C. Seymour et al. (Oxford, 1975–88), I.47–54. See below, section [22] in
the bibliography.

[12] Two printed versions of the *Informacio* appeared, in several editions, c. 1482–1510,
under the titles *Longe Parvula* and *Parvula.* The revised versions of *Accedence, Comparacio* and
Informacio (the last two now entitled *Gradus comparationum* and *Parvulorum institutio*) by John
Stanbridge are preserved in a total of 85 printings from the years 1505 to 1550. Cf. note
15 below. Just as the categories and terms of Latin grammar were applied to English in the
Middle English period, Latin rhetoric, in its traditional and contemporary form, played a
significant role in the composition of English literary texts of this period. [13]

c. 1050), the *Panormia* of Osbern of Gloucester (mid-twelfth century), the *Magnae Derivationes* of Hugutio of Pisa (c. 1200), the *Catholicon* of Johannes de Janua (completed around 1286), and also the *Summa*, with difficult biblical vocabulary, by William Brito (c. 1250). [25] All these were known and in use in late medieval England, the work by Hugutio being the most common of them. Scattered French and English interpretations in English copies of these dictionaries have yet to be studied.[13] By the fifteenth century, however, these dictionaries apparently no longer met the needs of all their potential English users; for many of them, the monolingual definitions may have been too difficult. As a result, the first bilingual dictionaries in the history of English were compiled, which naturally made generous use of their monolingual predecessors:

Latin-English: *Medulla Grammatice; Hortus Vocabulorum.*

English-Latin: *Promptorium Parvulorum; Catholicon Anglicum.*

Of these, the *Catholicon* is particularly noteworthy as it gives several Latin synonyms for very many of the c. 8,000 English entries, often together with explanations of their differences in meaning.[14] [27]

The Early Printers and Humanist Grammar

In their printing programs from the late fifteenth century onwards, the early printers included two of the dictionaries just mentioned (*Hortus* and *Promptorium*), along with collections of *Vulgaria,* and grammatical treatises in English that followed in the wake of John Leland; these especially included the books by John Stanbridge (died 1510), who from 1488 to 1494 was headmaster of the prestigious and influential school attached to Magdalen College, Oxford. Stanbridge, his predecessor John Anwykyll, Stanbridge's contemporaries and in particular his extremely productive

---

[13] On the dissemination of these dictionaries in England, see Bursill-Hall [7.2], the medieval library catalogues, and the *Registrum Anglie de libris doctorum et auctorum veterum,* ed. Richard H. Rouse and Mary A. Rouse, Corpus of British Medieval Library Catalogues, 2 (London, 1991), 227. —In this context, the great encyclopedias of the Latin Middle Ages should not be forgotten, notably the thirteenth-century *De proprietatibus rerum* by Bartholomaeus Anglicus, and the *Speculum maius* by Vincent of Beauvais. [26]

[14] The vocabularies and dictionaries of the late Middle English period still need a thorough study and listing. An example of what needs to be considered is the scarcely known Latin dictionary in MS. Trinity College, Cambridge, O.5.4 (1285), fols. 96–275, from the second quarter of the fifteenth century; of the c. 25,000 entries contained in it, at least a tenth are provided with explanations in English. See H. Gneuss, review of Gabriele Stein, *The English Dictionary before Cawdrey,* in *Anglia* 107 (1989), 481. An edition is now in progress.

pupil Robert Whittinton, together with the early English printers, are witnesses of the impact of the Humanist grammarians. The printers, who up to 1516 were still bringing out the *Doctrinale* of Alexander de Villa Dei and up to 1518 the *Synonyma* and *Equivoca* of John of Garland, published the *Opus grammaticum* of Johannes Sulpitius from 1494, while in Louvain an edition of Nicolas Perottus's *Rudimenta grammaticae* appeared with English annotations as early as 1486. The *De linguae Latinae elegantia* by Laurentius Valla was also known in late fifteenth-century England. It was on these works by Perottus and Valla, along with the *Doctrinale* of Alexander, that John Anwykyll based his *Compendium Totius Grammaticae,* printed at Oxford in 1483.[15] [28–29]

The Latin grammar of the Humanists, with its call for a return to classical Latinity, which found its way quite early to England, cannot be considered here, but mention must be made of the grammar which usually circulated under the name of William Lily. Proclaimed by Henry VIII the authorized textbook to be used all over the country, it dominated the teaching of Latin in England up to the eighteenth century. Its importance lay not only in the influence it exerted on Latin studies, for together with the grammars of the French scholar Petrus Ramus (*Grammatica,* 1559, and *Rudimenta Grammaticae,* 1559; both published in English translation in 1585), it became the basis of the early grammars of the English language. William Lily, who studied at Oxford and afterwards with Sulpitius in Italy, from 1510 to 1523 was High Master of St. Paul's School, London, which had been founded in 1509 by John Colet (c. 1476–1519; from 1504 Dean of St. Paul's). The publishing history of Lily's famous book is complicated. It was a joint effort; in the version printed since about 1540, the accidence (in English) was based on John Colet's *Aeditio,* while the syntax (in Latin) was by Lily, but had been revised by Erasmus. [29]

---

[15] Valuable information is available in booksellers' records. See the "Day-Book" of the Oxford bookseller John Dorne for the year 1520; among books on language sold most frequently, he listed Albertus, *De modis significandi;* Perottus, *Grammatica;* Sulpitius, *Grammatica;* L. Valla, *Elegantiae;* Stanbridge, *Opuscula, Parvula, Sum es fui, Vocabula, Vulgaria;* Whittinton, *Declinationes, De generibus nominum, Grammatica, Synonyma, Vulgaria,* and others. On this, and for references to English printed editions of the Humanists' works, see F. Madan, "The Daily Ledger of John Dorne, 1520," in *Collectanea,* First Series, ed. C. R. L. Fletcher (Oxford, 1885), 71–177. See also the account book of a Cambridge bookseller, only discovered in 1988: *Garrett Godfrey's Accounts c. 1527–1533,* ed. Elisabeth Leedham-Green, D. E. Rhodes, F. H. Stubbings, Cambridge Bibliographical Society Monograph, 12 (Cambridge, 1992), and the list of books printed 1492–1535 by Wynkyn de Worde in H. S. Bennett, *English Books and Readers 1475–1557,* second ed. (Cambridge, 1961), 239–76.

3. From the Renaissance to the End of the Eighteenth Century

The Status of English; Inkhorn Terms

In England, the grammatical description of English began in the late sixteenth century, and from this time onwards, English was studied in its own right, and no longer exclusively as an aid in the contrastive teaching of Latin. The period also saw the beginnings of the monolingual lexicography of English. Previous to this, however, a lively discussion had started on the status and use of English, which reflected the new role the language was now playing. We owe our knowledge of this controversy to the fact that it was carried on in the extensive printed literature of the period. [30]

Primarily, the debate hinged on the—real or alleged—imperfections of the English language, its lack of eloquence, its inferiority not only to the classical languages, but also to French, Italian, and Spanish. Comments of this sort occur in the works of Gavin Douglas, Sir Thomas Elyot, and the translator Arthur Golding; they go back to the time of the first English printer, William Caxton, and they refer mainly to the shortcomings of English prose and to the problems involved in translating from Greek and Latin. But the new sixteenth-century writings on arts and sciences as well as Elizabethan poetry and drama soon gave the lie to such judgments. Moreover, since the fifteenth century a new standard language had developed based on the dialect of London. What really mattered now was the proper use of the language: "Our tung is capable, if our people wold be painfull," wrote Richard Mulcaster in 1582 in his *Elementarie*. He was the first headmaster of the Merchant Taylor's School; we shall return to him shortly.

Linked to this debate in the sixteenth century was the dispute over 'inkhorn terms,' those numerous borrowings, mainly from Latin, which now entered the language. Often enough they served as useful technical terms, but in not a few cases they were employed as elements of an affected style of writing. Although many of these 'hard words' were short-lived, a considerable number have survived and still cause problems of style and comprehension even today, particularly, of course, for those with no knowledge of Latin, who therefore may not understand such words or misuse them. This development had its origins in the fourteenth century;[16] as late

---

[16] In *Piers Plowman* (B.v.232–36; C.vii.234–38), the word *restitucion* is misunderstood by Couetyse as meaning 'robbing people while they are asleep' (cf. *rest*), and in the morality

as 1619, Alexander Gill, in the preface to his *Logonomia Anglica,* reproached Chaucer for setting a bad example in this respect. Stephen Skinner made similar remarks in the foreword to his *Etymologicon Linguae Anglicanae* (1671), and already in 1490, Caxton had admitted in the prologue to his *Eneydos* that he had been criticized by some for making use, in his translations, of "over-curious terms which could not be understand of common people."[17]

The English language, however, continued to develop in its own way, and a large number of hard words remained. There were proposals to replace the foreign words with archaisms (as suggested by George Gascoigne in *The Posies,* 1575), or with new formations from native elements (as was advocated by Richard Puttenham and the logician Ralph Lever), but, like similar attempts in the nineteenth century, they were doomed to failure. Indeed, perceptive critics such as Thomas Wilson (*The Art of Rhetorique,* 1551) and Richard Mulcaster saw the usefulness of the new loanwords, yet they expressly condemned their unnecessary or misplaced use. A solution to the problem was attempted in the following century by the lexicographers.

From the seventeenth century, the status of the native language was no longer in doubt. English was now placed on an equal footing with foreign languages, both ancient and modern, and was even considered superior to them. The Puritans went further than this; their utilitarian ideas were linked to an appreciation of the virtues and potentialities of English, and as a consequence they aimed to reform the teaching of languages in schools, believing that too much time was expended on learning the classical languages, and thus calling into question the value of a Humanist education. In his *Academiarum Examen* (1653), John Webster, a clergyman and schoolmaster, likened the efficiency and usefulness of teaching and learning the classical languages to a carpenter taking seven years to prepare and sharpen his tools before using them.

---

play *Mankind* (c. 1465–70), Mercy is accused by New Gyse of being full of "Englysch Laten" (lines 122–24).

[17] Richard Verstegan refers to Chaucer as "a great mingler of English with French": *A Restitution of Decayed Intelligence* (Antwerp, 1605), 203.

Plans for an Academy

There was now a widespread belief that the English language was enjoying its 'Golden Age' in the sixteenth or seventeenth century. However, since up into the eighteenth century linguistic change was also seen by many as a process of decay, it seemed imperative to halt this by fixing the language, at the same time removing common corruptions and regulating any uncertainties of usage. It was thought that such work should be undertaken by an appropriate institution, an academy on the model of the Accademia della Crusca (founded in 1582) and the Académie Française (founded in 1634). When in the later eighteenth century the foundation of such an academy was mooted in North America, these institutions were once again held up as models.

The debate about the establishment of a language academy in the seventeenth and eighteenth centuries was not only carried on by those we might call the 'linguists' of the day—schoolmasters and authors of grammars and dictionaries—but also and especially by the leading figures of contemporary literature. The first plans came from the Royal Society (whose beginnings go back to the period around 1645). John Wilkins, Bishop of Chester from 1668 and a member of the Royal Society, published *An Essay towards a Real Character and a Philosophical Language* in 1668. Wilkins's *Essay* was the detailed project of an artificial, universal language and script based on philosophical principles, and at the same time an attempt—of which his is not the only instance in this period—to create a new, fixed and internationally intelligible language that would have the advantage "of facilitating mutual Commerce, amongst the several Nations of the World." As early as December 1664, the Royal Society had formed a "Committee for improving the English language." For various reasons, only three or four meetings were actually held before its work came to an end. However, one of the committee members, John Evelyn, wrote a letter to the chairman, Sir Peter Wyche, in which he outlined what even today must seem an astonishingly comprehensive and progressive plan of work for the committee, thus providing at the same time the most thorough description of the tasks which an English language academy would have to undertake, and of the books it would have to produce. These were: a prescriptive grammar; a reformed orthography; new punctuation marks and intonation symbols; a dictionary "of all the pure English words"; a collection of "technical words"; a kind of encyclopedia of weights and measures, coins and titles, national habits, etc.; a dictionary of foreign words; an inventory of the English dialects; a collection of phrases frequently used in conversation; alternative terms for archaisms and new expressions for concepts which at that time could only be named by means of foreign words; excerpts from ancient and modern orators and poets for the study of style; finally, original writings by members of the academy intended to serve as models. It will be clear from the above list that Evelyn's demands have not yet been fully met even by the linguists of the twentieth century.

Of other plans for a language academy, the best-known are those by Daniel Defoe (*Essay upon Projects,* 1698) and Jonathan Swift (*A Proposal for Correcting, Improving and Ascertaining the English Tongue,* 1712); further proposals came from John Dryden, Matthew Prior, and Joseph Addison. Defoe and Swift also wished to fix and regulate the English language: "what I have most at Heart is, that some Method should be thought on for ascertaining and fixing our Language for ever," said Swift. [31]

The opposing view, which regarded the idea of a regulated, unchanging language as wholly unrealistic, was, however, not new, at least not for those conversant with the history of the English language, such as Richard Verstegan and Meric Casaubon in the seventeenth century. By the later eighteenth century, this view had won general recognition, and two of the most intelligent minds of the period were expressly opposed to the idea of an academy, not only because it was unrealistic, but also because it was incompatible with the freedom of the individual. These two were the grammarian, theologian and scientist John Priestley (in the preface to his *Rudiments of English Grammar,* 1761), and the author, literary historian and lexicographer Samuel Johnson, who in 1747, in his *Plan of a Dictionary of the English Language,* had still considered the regulation of the language as feasible and desirable, but in 1755 expressly repudiated this opinion in the preface to his *Dictionary.*

In the end, nothing came of an English language academy, and the findings of historical philology in the nineteenth century were to show even more clearly how questionable the aims and arguments of the proponents of such an academy had been. Institutions founded from the nineteenth century onwards which might have assumed the function of an academy invariably turned to other tasks: the Royal Society of Literature (founded in 1825), the Philological Society (founded in 1842),[18] the British Academy (founded in 1902), the English Association (founded in

---

[18] For the early history of the Philological Society see pp. 46–48 and 50 below.

1907), and also the Modern Language Association of America (founded in 1883). The program closest to that of a language academy was proposed by the Society for Pure English, founded in 1913 by the poet Robert Bridges. He, however, expressly stated that the Society "absolutely repudiates the assumption of any sort of Academic authority or orthodoxy"; instead they wished to "organize a consensus of sound opinion which might influence and determine the practice of our best writers and speakers."[19]

The Reform of English Orthography and the Pronouncing Dictionary

The concrete tasks and achievements of English linguists from the sixteenth to the early nineteenth centuries lay above all in the areas of grammar, lexicography, and the reform of orthography; the impetus for such activities came—as will be seen—not so much from scholarly interest but rather from practical needs. A reform of English spelling had appeared urgent since the sixteenth century, as changes in pronunciation after the fourteenth century, particularly in the vowel system, and the loss of certain sounds were no longer reflected in the orthography—in direct contrast to earlier scribal practice. The reasons for this have never been fully explained; an important role may well have been played by the early printers. Whatever the reason, the result is a problem which has still not been solved today: when we read an English word, we cannot always be certain how it is pronounced; and conversely, when we hear a word spoken, we do not necessarily know how it is spelled. The existence of a large number of homophones serves only to aggravate the difficulties.

From the mid-sixteenth to the mid-seventeenth centuries, proposals were made for reform, initially by Sir Thomas Smith and Sir John Cheke, two Cambridge professors who had been inspired by the controversy over the pronunciation of Greek and Latin, in which they had favored the reformed (i.e., classical) pronunciation recommended by Erasmus in his *De recta Latini Graecique sermonis pronuntiatione* (1528).[20] At about the same time, John Hart published *An Orthographie* (1569), from a phonetician's

---

[19] Robert Bridges, *On English Homophones*, S. P. E. Tract no. II (Oxford, 1919), 46.

[20] A true reform of Latin pronunciation did not come about until the early twentieth century in England, and somewhat earlier in the USA; see W. Sidney Allen, *A Guide to the Pronunciation of Classical Latin*, second ed. (Cambridge, 1978), 102–10 and 128–29, and Thomas Pyles, *Selected Essays on English Usage* (Gainesville, Florida, 1979), 24–49.

point of view probably the soundest of the reform proposals, in which the author advocated a spelling system in which each sound would have only one corresponding letter. Other orthographic systems were devised by the early grammarians of English, William Bullokar (from 1580) and Alexander Gill (1619, 1621), by Charles Butler (1633)—who realized that English spelling reflected an older pronunciation of the language—and Richard Hodges (1643, 1644). The intense study of the relationship between writing and pronunciation led to an early occupation with questions of phonetics in England.[21] The reformers, however, met with no success in their endeavors. There was no authority to enforce the observance of their proposals; moreover, their spelling systems differed too widely from each other, and their use of diacritic signs and new letters to supplement the existing roman alphabet made their scripts unattractive. By contrast, Richard Mulcaster was more successful with his *First Part of the Elementarie* (1582), which also dealt with English orthography, but instead of aiming for a radical reform of the system he chose current usage as a foundation on which to base his cautious improvements, including in his book a list of over 8,000 words in the spellings he suggested; his work thus became a forerunner of the later 'spelling books'.

After the middle of the seventeenth century, little was heard about spelling reform for a long time. By the end of the seventeenth century English orthography had become fixed in all its essentials, and language critics in the eighteenth century such as Swift and Samuel Johnson expressly opposed a new system of spelling: apart from other problems, it would be at variance with the desired aim of fixing and standardizing the language. From the late eighteenth century, new attempts and proposals followed and continued into the present century, but all achieved little, if any, success. In England, the work of James Elphinston (from 1786) is worthy of note, and later, in the nineteenth century, that of Isaac Pitman, who also designed a new system of shorthand. In America, which was now beginning to play a role in the linguistic study of English, the first to argue for a reformed orthography were Benjamin Franklin (1768), and later, under his influence, the lexicographer and grammarian Noah Webster, who even enjoyed some limited success. In the latter decades of the nineteenth century various societies in favor of spelling reform were founded in Britain and America, and now gained the support of the most

---

[21] See below, pp. 55–57.

distinguished philologists of the period, such as Ellis, Sweet, Furnivall, Murray, and Skeat; in England, The Simplified Spelling Society, founded in 1908, is still active today. Again, nothing was achieved, nor was anything achieved later by George Bernard Shaw, who had offered a prize for a new English alphabet. But it should also be remembered here that weighty arguments for the preservation of the old spelling were advanced, notably by Henry Bradley (1913), one of the editors of the *Oxford English Dictionary,* who pointed out that the function of the visual image of the written word as a whole was more important than that of its individual letters. [32]

At least a partial solution to the problem had been found much earlier by other means, namely in the form of the pronouncing dictionary. Up into the eighteenth century, English dictionaries had not given any information on how words were pronounced. From 1723, some—such as the dictionary of Dr Samuel Johnson (1755)—began to mark the stress in polysyllabic words (a few bilingual dictionaries had done this earlier). Not long afterwards, the first of a series of dictionaries was published in which for every word entered the pronunciation was recorded; this was James Buchanan's *Linguae Britannicae Vera Pronunciatio* (1757). The best-known and most influential of these dictionaries, after Thomas Sheridan's *General Dictionary of the English Language* (1780), was the *Critical Pronouncing Dictionary* (1791, 1797, and many further editions in the nineteenth century) by John Walker, an actor and teacher of elocution; his work constitutes a remarkable achievement, but at the same time reveals certain prescriptive tendencies by adapting the pronunciation of a number of words to their spelling. All these dictionaries employ phonetic scripts based on the roman alphabet but supplemented with diacritical marks and various typefaces (in Buchanan), or with numbers printed over the vowels (in Sheridan and Walker).[22] Even today, some British and American dictionaries use similar methods of transcription; the international phonetic alphabet introduced in the late nineteenth century has by no means gained full acceptance in the English dictionary. What has, however, become common practice since the early nineteenth century for every entry in a general dictionary of English is the indication of stress and pronunciation. [33]—It may be noted at this point that the orthography problem has also posed serious difficulties for those who designed English shorthand systems since the late sixteenth century. [46]

---

[22] For the dictionary of Thomas Spence see below, p. 57.

The Grammar of English; the Rhetoricians

Of all the fields in the history of linguistic scholarship discussed here, the one most thoroughly explored is probably that of English grammar from the late sixteenth to the early nineteenth century. [34] More than 270 grammatical treatises dealing with English were published up to the end of the eighteenth century, and while they may not have been exhaustively studied, the ground has been covered in important work, especially by Otto Funke, Ivan Poldauf, Emma Vorlat and Ian Michael. I will therefore limit myself here to a few general remarks.

Of the 273 grammatical treatises listed and treated by Michael, two are still products of the sixteenth century (the grammars of Bullokar, 1586, and Greaves, 1594), less than thirty belong to the seventeenth century (to which we should add the proposals for universal languages), and a little more than thirty to the first half of the eighteenth century. More than two hundred, however, were written in the second half of the eighteenth century. These figures may be explained by the fact that English grammar was included only very late in the curricula of the grammar schools. Yet there is evidence to show that attention had been paid to English grammar and style long before Bullokar, in schools and elsewhere. This can be seen from the fifteenth century onwards in the above-mentioned Latin-English textbooks, and from the mid-sixteenth century in the manuals of rhetoric dealing with English usage, such as the well-known book by Thomas Wilson, *The Arte of Rhetorique* (1553). But in contrast to the elementary schools (the 'petty schools,' as they were called in the seventeenth century), which taught only the reading and writing of English, the curriculum of the grammar schools—well into the nineteenth century—was dominated by the teaching of Latin and, to a lesser extent, of Greek. Thus the grammars of the sixteenth and seventeenth centuries were primarily intended for foreigners learning English, and for this reason some of them were written in Latin, as for instance those by Paul Greaves (1594), Alexander Gill (1621), John Wallis (1653), and Christopher Cooper (1685). There was clearly a need for foreign language textbooks of this kind, particularly among the Huguenot refugees who had fled to England, as can also be seen from grammars and conversation manuals written by foreigners such as Jacques Bellot, Claudius Holyband, John Florio, George Mason, Paul Festeau and Guy Miège, all living in England at this time. Another aim of the grammarians from early times had been to prepare their English pupils for learning Latin: educational reformers such as Roger Ascham, Richard

Mulcaster, and their successors demanded that the teaching of language and grammar should begin with what was familiar, the mother tongue. Also, the contrastive method of teaching Latin had numerous exponents in the seventeenth and eighteenth centuries, such as John Brinsley with his *Ludus literarius* (1612). In the eighteenth century, grammars of English were mainly textbooks intended for English teachers and pupils, but also for adults wishing to improve their ability to express themselves in their native tongue.

Apart from occasional remarks or introductory chapters dealing with the history of English, the English grammarians up to the early nineteenth century were invariably concerned with the language of their own period. Some of the early authors combined their descriptions of the language with attempts to reform the orthography; Bullokar's grammar and Gill's English examples were actually printed in their new, reformed spelling. Most of the books contain the following sections: *orthography,* dealing with letters, sounds and syllables; '*etymology,*' since the late Middle Ages in the sense of inflection, and word-formation, of the parts of speech, and often including certain areas of syntax (especially in the chapters on pronoun, verb, and preposition); *syntax,* which due to the uninflected nature of English was often held to be less important, since government and concord play only a subordinate role in English, or none at all, while at this time the analysis of sentence structure was as yet insufficiently developed; finally, *prosody,* which deals with stress and metrics. In addition, there might be chapters on punctuation and rhetorical tropes and figures, as well as lists of homophones and homographs. In general the content and structure of these grammars was as varied as it is today; Ian Michael has found no less than 56 different types of arranging the parts of speech, and grammars which even today are accorded scholarly status, such as those of Wallis (1653) or Priestley (1761), say very little about syntax.

There is not much point in judging the early grammars and dictionaries by the standards of our own time. Unfortunately, in recent years they have come in for a good deal of anachronistic criticism. Like grammarians of almost all periods, the English authors of the sixteenth, seventeenth and eighteenth centuries combined their own judgments and observations with features taken from their immediate predecessors and with traditional elements that go back for centuries. Such is the case with the grammars by Christopher Cooper (1685), James Greenwood (1711) and Charles Gildon (1711), which follow more or less closely the *Grammatica Linguae Anglicanae* by John Wallis (1653), and with Lindley Murray's *English Grammar* (with numerous editions from 1795 onwards), based on the *Short Introduction to*

English Grammar by Robert Lowth (first published in 1762).

The English (and Scottish) grammarians of our period derived their descriptive categories and their terminology from Latin grammar. They have often been reproached for this by later critics, as already by William Hazlitt in *The Atlas* (15 March 1829) and G. F. Graham in the *Classical Museum* (1845). Such criticism has overlooked the fact that Latin offered the only grammatical model then available, and that for foreigners (and English speakers) who had learned or who were learning Latin the familiar grammatical categories of Latin could be of considerable help in the study of English. Moreover (though contemporary grammarians were not aware of this), the common origin of the two languages meant that, despite the development of English into an analytical language, structurally they were still related. A description of English using or adapting the categories and terms of Latin grammar was therefore possible, and—within reasonable limits—is still possible today, even if many may prefer not to admit this. Above all, however, such criticism ignores the fact that the problems arising from the use of Latin categories were more or less clearly recognized by many of the seventeenth- and eighteenth-century English grammarians, and solutions were sought for them. Thus, the scholarly reputation enjoyed by the *Grammatica Linguae Anglicanae* of John Wallis (from 1649 Professor of Geometry at Oxford, and a founder member of the Royal Society) in the late seventeenth and eighteenth centuries can surely be attributed to the fact that the author of this first truly scientific description of English, taking a critical look at the rules given in earlier grammars for case, gender and declensions of nouns, for tenses, moods and conjugations of verbs, and for government, described them all as "multa inutilia praecepta," and dismissed them in favor of a descriptive method more suited to the structure of English. Although Wallis's successors did not usually proceed with the same level of consistency—and made in fact quite a few mistakes—it would seem unreasonable to deny that in general they were rather well aware of the structural characteristics of their language. [35]

The grammarians of the seventeenth and eighteenth centuries had another reason for using 'Latin' categories, namely the idea that the different languages had a common foundation, and that it was the task of a universal grammar to describe this. Such a notion had been proposed by the speculative grammarians of the Middle Ages and subsequently, in England, by Francis Bacon. This theory was the basis of linguistic works which had a considerable influence on the English grammarians: on the one hand, the famous *Grammaire générale et raisonnée* by Antoine Arnauld and Claude Lancelot (1660), a product of the schools of Port-Royal (a Cistercian abbey near Paris, after which the grammar usually takes its name), which also appeared in an English translation in 1753; on the other hand, the above-mentioned attempts to create an artificial universal language, which in England were mainly confined to the two decades between 1647 and 1668, and whose crowning achievement in terms of structure, perfection and influence was the philosophical language of John Wilkins (1668). Each of these universal languages had to provide for a system of syntactic relations between its elements (and the various symbols used in writing); the system thus assumed the character of a universally valid grammar. An influential, systematic treatment of universal grammar is to be found later in James Harris's much-read *Hermes* (1751). [36–37]

English grammarians, especially those of the eighteenth and nineteenth centuries, have been accused of employing prescriptive methods. From the 1920s, this charge has been leveled in particular against the influential and successful grammars of the later eighteenth century[23] with their numerous editions and revisions, such as Robert Lowth's *A Short Introduction to English Grammar* (1762) and Lindley Murray's *English Grammar* (1795). Others have also come in for criticism, although rather less so in the case of Joseph Priestley's *The Rudiments of English Grammar* (1761). Such sweeping judgments have gained popularity in histories of English and of English grammar, but fortunately, in the light of more recent scholarship, they have been revealed as anachronistic and in need of revision; more research needs to be done in this area.

In fact, the English grammarians of this period do give a large number of rules, but the majority of these are concerned not so much with grammar in the narrower sense, but with style and the use of individual words. As the criteria for their decisions they often name reason, logic, analogy, etymology, or the example of the classical languages. Yet on closer examination these rules turn out to be isolated individual points in what is otherwise a generally descriptive approach to the grammar of English. There can be no doubt either that in many cases the grammarians did not exercise their subjective judgment but instead took as their guide the common usage of well-written prose. To reach satisfactory conclusions on this question, thorough comparative investigations will need to be made of

---

[23] Such criticism also occurred much earlier, for instance in the fourth of Noah Webster's *Dissertations on the English Language* (Boston, 1789).

contemporary texts and grammars. The fact that in the past such work has not always been done, or has not been based on sufficient evidence, is shown in the controversy over *shall* and *will* as markers of the future in English. It is the grammarians of the seventeenth and eighteenth centuries who have been confirmed in their requirement of *shall* for the first person and *will* for the second and third persons, and not the historical linguists of the twentieth century.[24] [38a] One also needs to consider the linguistic situation in the eighteenth century, as well as the aims of the grammars and the audiences for which they were intended: in a period in which English grammatical usage was often enough still variable and uncertain—for instance in morphology, especially as regards the strong verbs—grammarians were expected to remain true to the definition of 'grammar' usually given at the beginning of their books, namely that grammar is the art of speaking and writing correctly. In future, it may seem more appropriate to speak of prescriptive tendencies rather than of prescriptive English grammar in the eighteenth century and later. [38]

In the second half of the eighteenth century, language rules increasingly followed actual usage. This can also be seen in a discipline which now came to form a close connection with grammar, namely rhetoric. The old classical art of oratory, which had undergone a revival in the English Renaissance, was now replaced by the 'new' rhetoric, a comprehensive treatment of style which aimed to serve for all genres of spoken and written texts. Placing less emphasis than before on tropes and figures, the new rhetoric deals in particular with such features as the choice of words, sentence structure, paragraphs, sound and rhythm; *perspicuity* and *precision* are the most desirable qualities of a perfect style, and writers are to be guided by contemporary usage. The leading exponents of the movement were two Scottish professors, George Campbell, who, in his *Philosophy of Rhetoric* (1776, and over forty reprints in the nineteenth century), defined good usage as "reputable, national and present" (II.i), and Hugh Blair, who, in his *Lectures on Rhetoric and Belles Lettres* (1783, and at least 130 editions until 1911), formulated the basic principle: "Perspicuity, it will be readily admitted, is the fundamental quality of style" (Lecture X). What is here termed 'rhetoric' is reminiscent of Quintilian and his *consensus eruditorum* (*Institutio*

---

[24] The fact that the grammarians describe usage, rather than trying to influence or prescribe it, has also been shown in a study of the English relative pronoun in the seventeenth and eighteenth centuries by Marianne Knorrek, *Der Einfluss des Rationalismus auf die englische Sprache* (Breslau, 1938), 57–64.

oratoria, I.vi.45) rather than the rhetoric of the traditional manuals, and indeed Quintilian is referred to by both Blair and Campbell. [39]

"Perspicuity, precision, harmony (or the agreeable musical sound of the words when well pronounced)" and "figurative expression" are also the standards which John Priestley had already propounded in 1761 in his "Observations on Style" at the end of his *Rudiments of English Grammar*. It must be admitted that subjective judgments and prescriptive tendencies can be found in the works of Campbell and Blair. Nevertheless they laid important foundations for stylistics and literary criticism in the nineteenth century, and thus also for the many handbooks of usage and composition which have played a significant part in the study and teaching of Modern English since the nineteenth century.

Early Dictionaries to Johnson

English dictionaries even more than grammars reflect the development of the language, and the historical conditions under which they were written; both these factors affected the origin and spread of dictionaries as well as their contents. It seems possible to argue that in no other linguistic genre can progress in method be observed so clearly, despite occasional lapses and wrong turnings that occur on the way. The methodical achievements of English lexicography become apparent in the structure, size and aims of the dictionaries, the arrangement of the individual entries, and the phonetic, morphological, semantic, syntactic and stylistic information they offer.

The lexicography of English was at first exclusively bilingual, as has been shown above in the section on the fifteenth-century books. The emphasis of the sixteenth century was still on Latin-English (and English-Latin) dictionaries. The main aim now, however, was to record the usage of the classical Roman authors, as in Sir Thomas Elyot's *Dictionary* of 1538, which represents a decisive step forward in lexicographical method, and which was followed by other dictionaries, including Thomas Cooper's *Thesaurus linguae Romanae et Britannicae* (1565) and Thomas Thomas's *Dictionarium linguae Latinae et Anglicanae* (1587). In these, the great dictionary authorities of the Continent, notably Ambrogio Calepino and Robert Estienne (Stephanus), were used and drawn on freely. A tradition also started with the early lexicographers in England, which has continued in English dictionaries until the present day, particularly in those published in America: encyclopedic materials, especially proper names, are often included in the lexicon, thus obscuring the dividing line between language dictionary and encyclopedia.

The sixteenth century also saw the development of the first bilingual dictionaries of English and the modern European languages. Not surprisingly, French was the first to be so treated, in the dictionary section of John Palsgrave's *Lesclaircissement de la langue Francoyse* (1530: English-French), and in *A Dictionarie French and English* (printed in 1570 or 1571), perhaps by Claudius Holyband. In 1591 the first Spanish-English(–Latin) dictionary appeared, Richard Percyvall's *Bibliotheca Hispanica,* and in 1598 the first Italian-English dictionary, John Florio's *A Worlde of Wordes.* Dictionaries of Dutch (Henry Hexham, 1647–48) and German followed much later; it was only in 1706 and 1716 that Christian Ludwig's English-German-French and German-English dictionaries were published in Leipzig. [40]

In producing such dictionaries, the lexicographers and printers were clearly filling a genuine need, for their works ran through numerous new editions (in general I mention here only the first editions). This need was also met by a type of book which, while it would raise various methodical objections today, was extremely successful in the sixteenth and seventeenth centuries, namely the multilingual dictionary (mostly with three languages) and in particular the polyglot dictionary, which could cover up to ten or more languages. The authors of such works evidently had two types of users in mind, depending on whether the primary language of their dictionary was Latin, in which case it was to be of use to readers of different mother tongues for the study of Latin texts, or whether the book started from one of the modern languages, in which case it would serve the practical needs of sailors and travelers, although one must be wary of simplification in defining the readership of such books. Examples of the trilingual dictionary are the *Dictionariolum puerorum tribus linguis Latina, Anglica & Gallica scriptum* (1552, an enlarged revision of the Latin-French dictionary by Robert Estienne, 1544), and *An Alvearie or Triple Dictionarie, in Englysh, Latin and French* by John Baret (1573; in the edition of 1580 Greek was also included). Far more scholarly and wider-ranging than these, however, was the *Ductor in Linguas,* or *Guide into Tongues,* by the language teacher John Minsheu. Published in 1617, it contained over 12,000 entries, each English word being provided with its etymology (Minsheu was familiar with Old and Middle English) and its equivalent in ten languages: Welsh, Dutch, German, French, Italian, Spanish, Portuguese, Latin, Greek, and Hebrew. The book, which is also typographically a remarkable achievement, was intended by its author for both practical and scholarly purposes. It should be noted that this type of dictionary had forerunners in polyglot vocabularies such as a vocabulary in six languages, including English and German, published at Augsburg around 1530(?). Comprehensive polyglot dictionaries from the Continent, such as the revised edition of an earlier book by the well-known Ambrogio Calepino, published at Lyon in 1585 (*Dictionarium decem linguarum,* which included English), were known in England and certainly served as models. [41]

The earliest monolingual dictionaries of English owe their origin to the desire to make the 'hard words' comprehensible. This is the purpose of the dictionaries by Robert Cawdrey (1604), John Bullokar (1616), Henry Cockeram (1623), Thomas Blount (1656), Edward Phillips (1658) and Elisha Coles (1676). They were thus intended for native speakers and covered only a portion, albeit a continually expanding one, of the total English lexis. While Cawdrey's first edition contained 2,533 entries, Cockeram already had as many as 5,835, and Phillips about 11,000. The term 'hard words' here had a rather wider meaning than it has today; it included not only Latinisms, explained by (more common) synonyms or by paraphrases, but also technical terms and archaisms, such as words taken from Chaucer. From Bullokar onwards, encyclopedic entries are also found, and Cockeram places these in a separate section of his book. Blount adds etymologies to his definitions (which of course reflect the current state of etymological knowledge) and references to his sources, while Coles includes dialect and cant words.

As is to be expected in view of contemporary lexicographical practice, the seventeenth-century hard word dictionaries are not, in the strict sense, original works. Not only did they borrow words and entries from each other, their compilers also drew on Latin-English dictionaries and on glossaries of technical terms and archaisms from the sixteenth century. They also had their immediate predecessors: an incomplete, late-sixteenth-century handwritten draft of a dictionary of hard words has recently been discovered, and *The English Schoole Master* (1596) by Edward Coote, a textbook on orthography, with a catechism, contains a vocabulary of about 1,400 hard words with explanations, which not long afterwards was used by Cawdrey for his *Table Alphabetical.*

The decisive step from a collection of more or less difficult or rare words to a full-fledged English dictionary was made at the beginning of the eighteenth century by John Kersey in *A New English Dictionary* (1702), in which he aimed to produce a "Collection of all the most proper and significant *English* Words, that are now commonly us'd either in Speech, or in the familiar way of Writing Letters, etc.," and to combine the tradition of the hard word dictionary with that of the spelling book, a common type of textbook in England (and later in America), which we owe to the orthography problem. While Kersey's book still provides largely unsatisfactory definitions for 'ordinary words,' nevertheless, from now on English lexicographers saw it as their task to record as completely as possible the vocabulary of the language. This is not the place to list all the authors' names and the titles, editions and revised issues of their books. Mention should be made, however, of the most important eighteenth-century lexicographer in England before Johnson, Nathaniel Bailey, schoolmaster at Stepney, whose *An Universal Etymological English Dictionary* (1721) contained an amazing total of about 40,000 entries; his later *Dictionarium Britannicum* (first edition 1730) ran to about 60,000 words in the edition of 1736.

Long before Kersey and his successors, however, an admirable complete dictionary of English had appeared which until recently has been strangely neglected by historians of English lexicography. This was *An Alphabetical Dictionary Wherein all English Words According to their Various Significations Are either referred to their Places in the Philosophical Tables Or explained by such Words as are in those Tables,* compiled by William Lloyd to form part of John Wilkins's *Essay towards a Real Character* (1668). Obviously not intended as a practical reference work, it was, nevertheless, methodically far in advance of other contemporary English dictionaries.

Like the grammarians, the lexicographers of the eighteenth century now felt called not only to explain the vocabulary of English but also to regulate and fix its usage. Their predecessors in the seventeenth century had paid less attention to this question. Yet Cawdrey, in his foreword, (without giving his source) had printed Thomas Wilson's warning to his countrymen "that they never affect any strange inckhorne terms," whereas Bullokar and Cockeram were more inclined to encourage the use of hard words. Cockeram in the second part of his *Dictionarie* even had an alphabetical list of 'vulgar words' in English; for each of these he provides corresponding expressions which could be used in "more refined and elegant speech." Later, from 1658, the leading English lexicographers, Phillips, Kersey, Bailey and Benjamin Martin, began to mark any words they considered objectionable, particularly hard words, but also archaic and foreign vocabulary, dialect expressions, and 'low words'. In a sense then, these authors also supported, albeit in a rather unsystematic manner, the aims of those who were advocating the foundation of a language academy.
[42]
Completely new standards were finally set by Samuel Johnson's master-

piece *A Dictionary of the English Language,* which is mainly based on excerpts from important literary texts, particularly of the seventeenth century;
these excerpts were made according to the instructions given by the
widely-read author to his amanuenses. [43] Although, as in the work of his
predecessors, there is not yet any guidance to pronunciation (apart from
accents to mark stress), and although syntactic use is not indicated, the
arrangement and definitions of meanings show a degree of perfection
which is remarkable for the eighteenth century; thus, for the verb *to take,*
no less than 134 different meanings and idiomatic uses are listed. Johnson
also introduced into the lexicography of English the new method of illus-
trating the words and their meanings with quotations from literature; a
total of about 118,000 quotations occur in the two-volume dictionary
published in 1755. Johnson's dictionary went through numerous new and
revised editions until well into the nineteenth century, and must be regarded as one of the great classics of English linguistics; this applies in particular
to the famous "Preface" in which he explained the methodical principles
of his lexicographical work and discussed the problems he had encoun-
tered. What Dr Johnson has to say here has retained almost all its usefulness and relevance for modern lexicographers, notably also because he
had abandoned his original intentions (put forward in his *Plan for a Dictionary of the English Language* of 1747) after realizing that language cannot be
fixed and the process of linguistic change cannot be halted:

> Those who have been persuaded to think well of my design, will
> require that it should fix our language, and put a stop to those
> alterations which time and change have hitherto been suffered to
> make in it without opposition. With this consequence I will
> confess that I flattered myself for a while; but now begin to fear
> that I have indulged expectation which neither reason nor expe-
> rience can justify. When we see men grow old and die at a cer-
> tain time one after another, from century to century, we laugh
> at the elixier that promises to prolong life to a thousand years;
> and with equal justice may the lexicographer be derided, who
> being able to produce no example of a nation that has preserved
> their words and phrases from mutability, shall imagine that his
> dictionary can embalm his language, and secure it from corrup-
> tion and decay, that it is in his power to change sublunary
> nature, and clear the world at once from folly, vanity, and
> affectation.

Special Dictionaries; the Study of Language

English dictionaries from the sixteenth to the eighteenth centuries bear witness of the manifold linguistic interests of the period. Besides the monolingual and bilingual dictionaries of the general language, there were already dictionaries of a more specialist nature, which appear quite modern in their aims and approaches. We have already noticed the pronunciation and polyglot dictionaries; others can only be mentioned briefly. As early as 1570, Peter Levins published the first English rhyming dictionary, with Latin equivalents (*Manipulus Vocabulorum*); the first dialect dictionary, John Ray's *A Collection of Words not Generally Used*, appeared in 1674, and the first dictionary of cant, or thieves' slang (by a certain "B. E."), in about 1690. Historical and etymological dictionaries will be discussed below. The eighteenth century was a period in which the natural sciences increasingly gained in importance and prestige alongside the humanities; it was also the age of the first modern encyclopedias. These include the *Lexicon Technicum; or An universal English dictionary of the arts and sciences* by John Harris (first published 1704–10), the *Cyclopaedia* by Ephraim Chambers (first edition 1728), which became a model for the French *Encyclopédie,* and later the *Encyclopaedia Britannica* (first published 1768–71). [44]

One type of dictionary deserves special mention, for its development has to be seen—though not exclusively so—in connection with the enrichment of the English vocabulary by means of borrowing, especially through the hard words. This is the dictionary of synonyms, of which the first example in English was John Trusler's *The Difference between Words Esteemed Synonymous* (1766), which was followed by an unbroken series of successors until the present day. The treatment of synonymy has a long tradition and eventually goes back to the books on *differentiae* (including synonyms and homonyms) in classical antiquity. In the Middle Ages in England, this tradition of handbooks explaining Latin synonyms was continued. The pertinent works by Isidore of Seville, especially the *Libri differentiarum,* were available and were succeeded by Bede's *De orthographia,* by works of other English authors (Alcuin, John of Garland), and by vocabularies of the late Middle English period. Later on we have the numerous printed editions of the English-Latin version of the *Synonymorum sylva* by Simon Pelegromius (from 1580). The main aim of the dictionaries of English synonyms from the eighteenth century onwards was of course to define semantic distinctions, but their authors also began to consider questions of style, as can be seen in their warnings against words not to be used in the standard language, like those given in Hester Lynch Piozzi's *British*

Synonymy (1794). In the nineteenth century, a new, but closely related type of dictionary was created, and came to be known as the 'thesaurus,' which systematically arranges the whole vocabulary of the living English language according to topics, but does not give definitions or explain semantic differences. Published in numerous new or revised versions, the thesaurus has enjoyed remarkably widespread popularity in English-speaking countries up to the present day. The founder of this tradition was Peter Mark Roget, a medical doctor and from 1827 Secretary of the Royal Society. Systems of classification in the natural sciences no doubt played a role when Roget planned and compiled his famous *Thesaurus of English Words and Phrases;* the first edition was published in 1852, the latest version in 1987. [45]

In my account of the history of the study of English from the Renaissance to the beginning of the nineteenth century, with which this chapter has been concerned, I have not been able to do full justice to the manifold interests and activities of English-speaking linguists. The limitations of this study precluded a treatment of the increase in the knowledge of foreign languages and of what was achieved in translations from various languages. Nor was it possible to chart the beginnings of shorthand and the early attempts at the teaching of the deaf and dumb. An account of the ideas on the origin and diffusion of languages might also have been given; the following chapter will examine the development of scholarly interest in the history of the language. For the English representatives of the philosophy of language in the period I must refer the reader to the relevant section of the Bibliography. The relations between English and continental linguistics up to the close of the eighteenth century would require a separate study, which still needs to be written.[25] [46]

4. The Nineteenth Century

The seventeenth and above all the eighteenth century laid the foundations of the descriptive grammar, stylistics and lexicography of the living English

---

[25] Here are just two examples of such links: John Hart was familiar with the efforts of the spelling reformers in France and had read the *Traité touchant le commun usage de l'escriture françoise* (1545) by Louis Meigret (see Hart, *An Orthographie,* fol. 53r); in his *Institutiones Grammaticae Anglo-saxonicae et Moeso-gothicae* (1689), George Hickes refers specifically to his knowledge and admiration of the Port-Royal grammar (1660) and the *Ausführliche Arbeit von der Teutschen Haubtsprache* by Justus Georg Schottel (1663).

language, foundations on which the nineteenth century was to build for some time to come. The continuity of the tradition is well seen in the fact that the books by Lowth and Lindley Murray, Blair and Campbell, Samuel Johnson and John Walker were still appearing in reprints and revised editions long after the turn of the century. Thus, as far as works intended to describe or teach the living language are concerned, it would make little sense to draw a clearly defined line between the eighteenth and nineteenth centuries. [47] Decisive changes only came about later on, especially under the influence of historical linguistics, to which we will now turn our attention.

The beginnings and early development of historical and comparative linguistics are inseparably linked to the names of Rasmus Rask, Jacob Grimm, Franz Bopp, and August Schleicher (to mention only the most important), and later to those of the so-called Neogrammarians. The efforts and achievements of all of them have been described and appraised many times and thus require no treatment here.[26] [48] But we have to ask to what extent their new insights influenced English language scholarship in the nineteenth century, now that it had become possible to study, on a sound scientific basis, the prehistory and the historical development of English as documented in written records.

Early Students of Old English

Those who first set about this task did not have to do so empty-handed. For more than two hundred years English scholars had done remarkable and wide-ranging preparatory work in this field. Before turning to the nineteenth century proper, we should examine their achievements.

From the late sixteenth century, the history, literature and language of the Anglo-Saxons had been the object of scholarly studies. It was not, however, the philological attraction of this work that led scholars to undertake it, but rather its historical and antiquarian value, and in particular its theological interest. Another impulse came from an enthusiasm for things Germanic that had arisen after the rediscovery of Tacitus's *Germania* (the first English translation of this text was printed in 1598). Such enthusiasm found its full expression in two publications of the same year (1605):

---

[26] It is well known that there were forerunners in the field of comparative and historical linguistics long before the nineteenth century. One of the earliest, Gerald of Wales, was mentioned above (p. 14). [49]

Remaines of a greater work concerning Britaine by William Camden, and *A Restitution of Decayed Intelligence in Antiquities concerning the most renowned English nation* by Richard Verstegan (a pseudonym for Richard Rowlands). Before this, two text editions had appeared with the express purpose of defending the religious tenets of the now independent Church of England. These editions were the work of Archbishop Matthew Parker and his circle: *A Testimonie of Antiquitie* (1566), which includes, among other texts, Ælfric's Easter homily (*Catholic Homilies* II.xv), as well as the Lord's Prayer, the Creed and the Ten Commandments in Old English, and *The Gospels of the fower Euangelistes* (1571) in the West-Saxon version. Further, more extensive editions of texts followed later, and it was on this basis that the nineteenth-century philologists were able to build. It should be noted, incidentally, that an overt anti-Catholic tendency is discernible in the work of the early editors even well into the eighteenth century.

The Anglo-Saxon language was held in great esteem by the antiquaries, but posed a number of serious difficulties for them. The sixteenth and seventeenth centuries thus saw the preparation of various works intended to provide access to this language; at first these were dictionaries, a grammar followed rather late. Only a few names and significant books can be mentioned here. As early as the 1570s, dictionaries were compiled by Laurence Nowell and John Joscelyn, Matthew Parker's secretary. These and others, apart from a list of more than 600 Old English words in Verstegan's *Restitution* (pp. 207–39), remained unpublished. The first published dictionary was the *Dictionarium Saxonico-Latino-Anglicum* (1659) by William Somner, the second scholar (after Abraham Wheloc) to hold the lectureship in Anglo-Saxon established by Sir Henry Spelman at the University of Cambridge. Somner's work was exemplary for its time and remained unsurpassed until well into the nineteenth century. The achievement of the early lexicographers is all the more remarkable when it is remembered that they had to work almost without any linguistic aids; it seems reasonable to assume that the extensively preserved Latin texts with Old English interlinear glosses were particularly valuable to them. It was obviously even more difficult to write an Anglo-Saxon grammar. Somner—who must have intended his work to serve as a general handbook of Old English—printed Ælfric's *Grammar* as the second part of his *Dictionarium,* along with a few notes ("Regulae Saxonicae") at the end of his preface which cannot in all fairness be described as a 'grammar'; these he took word for word from Wheloc's 1643 edition of the Old English translation of Bede and of the Anglo-Saxon Chronicle. [50]

In the course of the seventeenth century, texts and documents of the other early Germanic languages became known in England, among them especially the Gothic Bible. In 1665, Francis Junius (1589–1677), who lived in England for thirty years and who of all the early antiquarians may have had the most thorough knowledge of the Anglo-Saxon language, published his edition of the Gothic Bible in Holland; ten years prior to this, he had brought out the first edition of Old English biblical poems, ascribed by him to Cædmon. The first grammar of Old English, printed in 1689, was combined with a grammar of Gothic.[27] We owe this work to the only scholar of the time with a universal command of the early Germanic dialects, George Hickes (1642–1715), who later reedited this comparative grammar together with grammars of Old High German, Old Saxon and Icelandic (the latter by Runolphus Jonas) in his *Linguarum Vett. Septentrionalium Thesaurus Grammatico-Criticus et Archaeologicus* (1703–1705), a work which, with good reason, is still admired today. Part two of this collection contained the great catalogue of Anglo-Saxon manuscripts by Humphrey Wanley, which, just a short time after the publication of the pioneering work by Jean Mabillon, *De re diplomatica* (1681), established the foundations of palaeographic studies in England.[28] [51]

Hickes's Old English grammar could no longer meet the demands of historical linguists in the later nineteenth century, particularly in its treatment of the inflectional system, but this should not detract from the importance of his work, which extends well beyond the time in which it was written. It seems notable that all grammars of Old English published in the eighteenth century (such as that of Elizabeth Elstob, 1715, in English) were based on Hickes, and real progress in the description of the oldest stage of the English language was not made until more than a hundred years after Hickes in the work of Rask and Grimm. Finally, two instances should be given of the early general interest in Anglo-Saxon. In 1755, a professorship of Anglo-Saxon was founded at the University of Oxford (the chair was first filled in 1795). In America, Thomas Jefferson occupied himself with Anglo-Saxon as early as the 1760s, and introduced

---

[27] John Joscelyn had already written an Anglo-Saxon grammar in the late sixteenth century, but only its index survives. See M. S. Hetherington, *The Beginnings of Old English Lexicography* (1980), 47 and 186–88.

[28] It is regrettable that Wanley's magnificent achievement has so far been ignored in continental histories of palaeography; thus Ludwig Traube, in his *Vorlesungen und Abhandlungen,* I (Munich, 1909), 43, does not even name the author of the catalogue of manuscripts in Hickes's *Thesaurus.*

it as a subject of study, with a professorship, at the University of Virginia about 1819.

Early Students of Middle English; Early Histories of English; Etymological Dictionaries

In contrast to Old English, the language of the Middle English period was little studied before the nineteenth century; this is particularly true of the early Middle English texts of the twelfth and thirteenth centuries. The later Middle English authors, on the other hand, seemed to present fewer linguistic problems, and some of them, especially Chaucer, had become firmly established in the English literary canon. Yet the linguistic knowledge of the time remained inadequate for a full understanding of Chaucer's art. "The verse of Chaucer, I confess, is not harmonious to us," says John Dryden in the preface to his *Fables, Ancient and Modern* (1700); this demonstrates that late Middle English verse was no longer properly understood, because the loss of final syllables in English and the original stress on words of French origin were not taken into account. Nevertheless, the correct interpretation of Chaucer's verse came as early as 1775 in Thomas Tyrwhitt's introduction to his edition of the poet. Much earlier, John Wallis in his *Grammatica Linguae Anglicanae* (1653), p. 57, had realized the origin and significance of the "*e mutum*" in English. Already in the sixteenth century readers of Chaucer required help with the poet's vocabulary. Accordingly, Paul Greaves appended to his *Grammatica Anglicana* (1596) a list of 120 words from Chaucer which were either archaic or used in an archaic sense. Two years later, Thomas Speght listed and explained about 2,500 "old and obscure words of Chaucer" in his edition of the poet. Many of these words then found their way into the hard word dictionaries of the seventeenth century. [52]

How thoroughly some scholars knew their Middle English—long before the first Middle English grammar was published—can be seen in the case, well-known in literary history, of the *Rowley Poems* by Thomas Chatterton (about 1770). These were convincingly exposed as forgeries on the basis of linguistic criteria by Thomas Tyrwhitt (1778, 1782) and Thomas Warton (1782). [53]

Two pre-nineteenth-century types of work in historical linguistics remain to be mentioned, namely treatments of the history of English, and etymological dictionaries. The early historiography of English must not, of course, be judged by modern standards. The accounts of the development of English mainly took the form of brief introductions to grammars (for instance those of Gill, Wallis, Cooper, Miège, Gildon-Brightland) and to dictionaries (Phillips, Skinner, Bailey 1721, Johnson). They focussed on external historical events, on vocabulary, and on borrowing, and what they had to say about the genetic relationship of languages was hardly reliable.[29] Nevertheless, they demonstrate the interest of the early modern period in linguistic history and also, more generally, in the origin and spread of languages. This was accompanied by a fascination for things Germanic and Anglo-Saxon, typified by Camden, who in his *Remaines Concerning Britaine* (1605) praised among other things the ability of Old English to create loan-formations. With his inclusion in the book of various versions of the Lord's Prayer, he was the first to publish parallel texts in English from different periods. [54]

At first sight it seems rather surprising to find that etymological dictionaries of English could already be compiled in the seventeenth century. They included, of course, not a few erroneous and speculative interpretations, as their authors were still employing the ancient and medieval methods of explaining etymologies. On the other hand, they were also able to draw on a wealth of linguistic knowledge that had become available since the time of the Humanists. In fifteenth-century England, we can normally assume only a knowledge of French and Latin; in the following centuries, however, Greek, Hebrew, Spanish, Italian, German and Dutch became known to etymologists, along with Old and Middle English and other Germanic dialects. Etymologists could also take advantage of the insights of the great French Renaissance philologist Joseph Justus Scaliger (1540–1609), who had divided the European languages into eleven 'mother tongues' (*matrices linguae*) and their descendants; nevertheless, inept notions of the kinship of languages persisted. Such knowledge then was the basis of the etymological explanations in John Minsheu's *Ductor in Linguas* (who still believed in the theory of the Antwerp doctor Johannes Goropius Becanus that Dutch had been the original language of humanity, yet derived many English words from Hebrew). It also formed the basis of the etymologies in the dictionaries of Thomas Blount (1656) and Edward Phillips (1658), and in the specifically 'etymological' dictionaries (as they were entitled) of Stephen Skinner (1671) and Francis Junius (first published by Lye in 1773), and in the anonymous *Gazophylacium Anglicanum* (1689)

---

[29] A very similar treatment is the "History of the English Language" in Noah Webster's *Dissertations on the English Language* (Boston, 1789), I.40–79.

based on Skinner. The most scholarly of these, despite its weaknesses, is the *Etymologicon Linguae Anglicanae* by Skinner, a doctor in Lincoln (with a medical degree from the University of Heidelberg). In his "Prolegomena Etymologica" he already refers to regular laws governing the change of 'letters,' and he emphasizes the role of semantic change in etymology. He is also superior to Minsheu when he derives words from Old English. [55]

The Beginnings of the Historical Study of English

When the principles of historical and comparative linguistics were intro-duced into the study of English in the nineteenth century, the effects of the new methods were not, as may have been thought, limited to the field of the history of the language. Three major developments should be noted:

1. The stages in the historical development of English could now be analyzed thoroughly and reliably, and the living language could be explained historically throughout.
2. Grammarians and lexicographers learned from historical linguistics how to produce comprehensive and precise descriptions of the living language.
3. New linguistic disciplines developed.

I shall deal with each of these points in what follows.

With Jacob Grimm's *Deutsche Grammatik* (1822–37), a new foundation had been provided for the historical study not only of German, but also of English. It has sometimes been suggested that England was somewhat late in paying attention to the discoveries of Grimm, Rask, and Bopp, and that this recognition was at first merely sporadic. But there is only a limited truth in these complaints. It should be remembered that until well into the nineteenth century neither comparative linguistics nor English philology existed as university subjects. In England, the Rawlinson professorship of Anglo-Saxon at the University of Oxford was a notable exception, but it was not the holders of this chair who first welcomed and propagated the new field of studies. Instead, the task was taken on by two scholars with-out university posts, Benjamin Thorpe (1782–1870) and John Mitchell Kemble (1807–57), who applied the new methods to the study of Anglo-Saxon language and literature and produced editions of Old English texts some of which are still in use today. Thorpe had studied with Rask in Copenhagen from 1826 to 1830 and had published an English translation of Rask's Anglo-Saxon grammar in 1830. Kemble, a friend and admirer of Jacob Grimm and personally acquainted with the Munich philologists

Massmann, Schmeller and Thiersch, was a vehement critic of the current Anglo-Saxon studies at Oxford. The pioneering work of Kemble and Thorpe was published in the three decades from 1830 to 1861, and was thus contemporary with the work of another pioneering Anglo-Saxonist, Joseph Bosworth (1789–1876; from 1858 Rawlinson Professor at Oxford). His *Dictionary of the Anglo-Saxon Language* appeared in 1838; it included his "Essentials of Anglo-Saxon Grammar," which, in contrast to his *Elements of Anglo-Saxon Grammar* of 1823, now followed the model and method provided by Grimm. [56]

In this early period of the 1830s and 1840s, the new historical and comparative method found an audience in England not only among those interested in Anglo-Saxon.[30] Grimm's *Deutsche Grammatik* had become known there soon after its publication, and even before this, Franz Bopp had published in 1820 an English translation of a revised version of his book on the conjugation system of the Indo-European languages. The scholar who did the most to spread the ideas of Rask and Grimm in mid-nineteenth-century England was undoubtedly Robert Gordon Latham (1812–88), a philologist, ethnologist and medical scholar. From 1839 to 1845, Latham held the new chair (established in 1829) of English Language and Literature at University College, London; his book *The English Language* appeared in 1841, and a much enlarged edition in 1848 (fifth edition 1862). This was the first historical grammar and history of the English language based on scientific principles, albeit not yet a fully comprehensive and systematic treatment of these fields. In it, Latham discussed questions of general linguistics; he set forth Grimm's Law and, for purposes of comparison, included forms from other Germanic dialects and also from Middle English.

The Philological Society and *The Oxford English Dictionary*

An important mediator of the new philology was Max Müller (1823–1900), professor of modern languages at Oxford from 1854. His widely-read *Lectures on the Science of Language* appeared in 1861–64; in 1868 he became the first to hold the new Oxford chair of comparative philology.

---

[30] Among them was William Barnes, who became well-known as a dialect poet and as a linguistic purist; see Bernard Jones, "William Barnes (1801–1886): The New Philology and the Philological Society," *The Henry Sweet Society Newsletter*, 19 (Nov. 1992): 7–9, and Willis D. Jacobs, *William Barnes Linguist* (Albuquerque, New Mexico, 1952).

But well before English philology established itself as an academic discipline and university subject during the last four decades of the nineteenth century, philologists and others with a general interest in language had joined to found the Philological Society, an association which gave a decisive impetus to the new discipline. In the first decade and a half of its activities, English and its history played only a limited role in the lectures and publications of the Society, but right from the start its members gave full recognition to the progress and achievements of the comparative and historical method developed on the Continent. Thus, in the first volume of the *Proceedings of the Philological Association* we are told in a report of the meeting on March 24th, 1843: "Prof. F. Bopp of Berlin, and Professor James Grimm of Berlin, were elected Honorary Members of the Society." [57]

Shortly before the first great historical grammars of English were published, the Philological Society initiated the project that has become the indispensable foundation for all research into the history of English, namely *The Oxford English Dictionary,* or—as it was originally called—*A New English Dictionary on Historical Principles,* "the greatest dictionary of any language in the world" (A. C. Baugh). A key figure in the instigation of the project was Richard Chenevix Trench (1807–86), an erudite and widely-read theologian (1846–58 professor at King's College, London; 1856–63 dean of Westminster; 1863–84 archbishop of Dublin), who, before he became a member of the Philological Society in 1857, had already lectured to students on English word history (published as *The Study of Words,* first edition 1851, and *English Past and Present,* first edition 1855). Dissatisfied with the state of English dictionaries at the time, the Society had previously decided to produce a supplement to them. In November 1857, Trench read two papers to the Society, entitled "On some Deficiencies in our English Dictionaries," in which he expressed and documented—by means of numerous examples—his fair and objective criticism of what were then the standard dictionaries (Dr. Johnson's *Dictionary* as revised by Henry J. Todd and first published in 1818; Noah Webster, *An American Dictionary of the English Language,* 1828; Charles Richardson, *A New Dictionary of the English Language,* 1836–37). Trench's remarks focused on defects in their treatment of the history of words, which he illustrated mostly with examples from English literature of the sixteenth century and later.

This led to the decision, taken by the Philological Society in 1858, to create a completely new dictionary of the English language. Work began already in the following year under the editorship of Herbert Coleridge, and was continued after his early death (1861) under Frederick J. Furnivall (1825–1910); the task was finally taken on in 1879 by James A. H. Murray, the *Oxford Dictionary's* editor for decades, and later on by his colleagues and successors Henry Bradley (from 1889 Joint Editor), William Alexander Craigie and Charles Talbut Onions. Their dictionary is a magnificent achievement in terms of organisation and scholarship, offering its readers far more than Trench had envisaged: an exhaustive treatment of all English words still in use after the year 1100 with regard to their etymology, spelling, and history, their changes in both form and meaning. About six million quotations, collected by hundreds of volunteer readers, served as the basis for the dictionary, which was published in 125 fascicles between 1884 and 1928. Its typographic arrangement is to be considered as exemplary, and in this and other features it is clearly superior to Grimm's *Deutsches Wörterbuch,* which had begun to appear in 1854. [58]

The high standard of scholarship reflected in the *Oxford English Dictionary,* in the historical grammars and the histories of the English language published from the 1860s onwards, was largely due to the advances in method which historical linguistics had made in the few decades since its beginnings. In the majority of cases, it was now possible, on the basis of securely established laws of sound change, to ascertain the etymological origin and the cognates of a given word, and to determine its inflectional class and morphology; it was also possible to identify with certainty the loanwords in the language. However, a serious obstacle for the scholars working on the *Oxford English Dictionary,* on new Middle English dictionaries, and on historical grammars, was the fact that a large proportion of the medieval texts, particularly those in Middle English, were still unpublished and thus only accessible in medieval manuscripts. It was here that the organizational talent of the practical-minded Frederick Furnivall proved invaluable: in 1864 he founded the Early English Text Society, which energetically applied itself to editing unpublished texts. By the turn of the century more than 200 volumes had been printed (in 1995 there are 444 volumes, of which 42 contain Old English texts).

Histories of English; Historical Grammars; Etymology

The progress made by philologists in the course of the nineteenth century and (as we see it today) a certain optimism regarding their achievements must have made it appear possible and desirable to produce comprehensive treatments of the history of English. If we leave aside the early and relatively limited attempt by Latham, the first book of this kind is the historical grammar by a schoolteacher at Eisenach in Thuringia, Karl Friedrich Koch's three-volume *Historische Grammatik der englischen Sprache* (1863–69).[31] At about the same time, Eduard Mätzner, headmaster of the Luisenschule in Berlin, published his historically oriented *Englische Grammatik,* likewise in three volumes (1859–65). Slightly later are the comparable if shorter works by Richard Morris, also a schoolmaster—and distinguished editor of medieval English texts—(*Historical Outlines of English Accidence,* first edition 1871; *Elementary Lessons in Historical English Grammar,* 1874). These books constituted a decisive step forward: based on extensive source materials, they presented a systematic account of the development of English phonology and morphology, word-formation and syntax. They soon appeared in revised editions and had numerous successors. However, the works which followed them proved to be less comprehensive, or different in their approaches. This is true of the "Geschichte der englischen Sprache" by Friedrich Kluge, Dietrich Behrens and Eugen Einenkel in Hermann Paul's *Grundriss der germanischen Philologie* (first published in 1891), of the *Historische Grammatik der englischen Sprache* by Max Kaluza (1900–1901) and the well-known work with the same title by Karl Luick (whose first part was published in 1914); also of *A Short History of English* by Henry Cecil Wyld (first edition 1914), and later of *Die englische Sprache* by Karl Brunner (first published 1950–51). In the grammars—to be mentioned again below—by Henry Sweet (1891–98) and Otto Jespersen (from 1909), the historical sections provided the foundation for a treatment of the modern, living language. At the same time, a new type of history of English became increasingly common and popular; this dealt with the history of the language in a more general and discursive manner, paid attention to the historical background and included, to a certain extent, elements of historical grammar. Two American books of this type by professors at Yale and Cornell University are representative of the state of English philology at the end of the nineteenth century: Thomas Lounsbury's *History of the English Language* (first edition 1879), and Oliver F. Emerson's *The History of the English Language* (1894). They were followed several years later in Europe by two works that have become classics of the genre: Henry Bradley's *The Making of English* (1904), and Otto Jespersen's *Growth and Structure of the English Language* (1905).

---

[31] Another scholar before Koch, also a schoolteacher, had already made use of the historical grammars of Grimm and Friedrich Diez (the founder of Romance philology): Eduard Fiedler, *Wissenschaftliche Grammatik der englischen Sprache,* 2 vols (Leipzig, 1850–61), with Carl Sachs as co-author of vol. 2.

There were good reasons why the encyclopedically conceived historical grammar of English failed to find successors after Koch and Mätzner. Too many details were still missing in the story, for instance an adequate knowledge of medieval and modern English dialects, or a convincing explanation of the rise of the Early Modern English standard language. As a consequence, research in the history of English became characterized by investigations and treatments of individual periods or special fields—and has remained so to this day. A vista on what needed to be done had been opened up by the phonetician Alexander John Ellis in his five-volume *On Early English Pronunciation* (1867–89), which covered the history of English pronunciation and the modern dialects, while Eduard Sievers's *Angelsächsische Grammatik* (1882) became a model for future studies of the phonological and inflectional system of a particular period of the language. Also characteristic of the later nineteenth century were the many doctoral dissertations which were to make contributions to a full picture of the history of English still to be worked out.

It will have become clear from the above discussion that a major contribution to the study of English in the nineteenth century was made by scholars from the European Continent, especially (though not exclusively) by German-speaking philologists working in the fields of comparative linguistics and of English and German studies. In England, reference was frequently made to the importance of Grimm, and later to that of the Neogrammarians, who drew linguistics closer to the realm of science. This is seen particularly in the "Presidential Addresses," from the 1870s onwards, of the Philological Society, in which Henry Sweet, together with Ellis and Morris, Furnivall, Murray, and Skeat, had taken on a leading role. In his 1878 address, Sweet reported on editions of Old English texts by Richard Wülker and Julius Zupitza, on the first volumes of the new academic journals *Englische Studien* (from 1876, edited by Eugen Kölbing) and *Anglia* (from 1878, edited by Richard Wülker), and on research into the laws of *Auslaut* (providing the explanation for the development of the Germanic inflectional system) and Verner's Law. On the same occasion four years later, Sweet described Hermann Paul's *Prinzipien der Sprachgeschichte* (first edition 1880) as "The most important work on general philology that has appeared of late years," and stressed the need of a knowledge of Indo-European for those working in the field of Old English. For Sweet, as for the Neogrammarians, it is the regularity of sound change and the operation of analogy that form the basis for an explanation of linguistic developments, while the observation of the living language was felt to be essential for a true understanding of language change.

Similar principles were followed by the great English historical linguists of the period: James Murray, Henry Bradley, Joseph Wright, and Walter William Skeat. From 1878 the first Elrington and Bosworth Professor of Anglo-Saxon at Cambridge, Skeat (1835–1912)—who produced numerous editions of medieval English texts, including the first critical editions of the West-Saxon Gospels and of the works of Chaucer and Langland—finally placed the study of English etymology on a sound scientific basis with his *Etymological Dictionary of the English Language* (first published 1879–82), which was also intended to support the work on the *Oxford English Dictionary,* and with his *Principles of English Etymology* (1887–91). In both books, he set forth his 'canons' for etymological research. This seemed necessary, even at this late date, because outside the small circle of competent philologists, unreliable and absurd etymologies were still being put forward well into the nineteenth century. Representative examples can be found in the dictionaries by Noah Webster (in editions before 1864) and Charles Richardson (1836–37), and in the *Imperial Dictionary* by John Ogilvie (first edition 1850), which was largely based on Webster's work. The influential book by Horne Tooke, *Epea pteroenta or the Diversions of Purley* (1786–1805), also enjoyed a longstanding high regard in England. Written in opposition to James Harris's *Hermes* and its idea of a universal grammar, it recognized quite early the value of historical methods in linguistics, but unfortunately its etymologies were largely incorrect.[32]

English in the Universities; the Study of Modern English

In general, it may be said that great and decisive steps forward were made in English language scholarship during the last few decades of the nineteenth century and the subsequent period, and that they were made predominantly, though not exclusively so, in the area of historical linguistics. It is important to remember that some of the most highly esteemed

---

[32] The lectures of Edward Newenham Hoare, *English Roots: And the Derivation of Words from the Ancient Anglo-Saxon,* second ed. (Dublin, 1856), give an idea of the etymological knowledge of the period. Basing himself on authorities like Verstegan and Horne Tooke, he declares, for instance, that *connect* and *knit* are related words. A fair and competent appraisal of the controversial work by Horne Tooke is given by Walter W. Skeat, *Principles of English Etymology. Second Series* (Oxford, 1891), 449–50.

historical linguists of the time had turned their attention also to the living language and to the teaching of languages, and had published significant contributions to these fields. By far the most distinguished and influential of them was Henry Sweet; special mention should also be made of Otto Jespersen and Wilhelm Viëtor (professor of English philology at Marburg from 1884), as well as of Arnold Schröer, and, from the younger generation of professors of English in Germany, Max Deutschbein, Heinrich Spies and Karl Wildhagen.

The advances in the study of English must also be seen in the context of the introduction of the modern languages into the curricula of the universities. In England, the older chairs of Anglo-Saxon at Oxford and Cambridge, and the chair at University College, London, were now followed by professorships of English language at Manchester (first held by T. Northcote Toller, from 1880) and Liverpool (first incumbent H. C. Wyld, from 1904). In 1885 the Merton Professorship of English Language and Literature was established at Oxford; it was first held by A. S. Napier, who had previously taught in Berlin and Göttingen. In the universities of the United States, important events in our field were the appointments of Francis James Child as professor of English at Harvard University (1876) and of his pupil and colleague George Lyman Kittredge at the same university in 1895; in 1889 Albert Stanburrough Cook joined his colleague Thomas R. Lounsbury as professor at Yale University. All over the German-speaking countries, chairs of English philology had been established at the universities by the end of the nineteenth century; among the first were those at Strasbourg (1872: Bernhard ten Brink), Leipzig (1875: Richard Paul Wülker), Berlin (1876: Julius Zupitza), and Vienna (1876: Jakob Schipper). It is well-known that many of the leading early exponents of English language studies in England and America had studied historical and comparative linguistics at German universities; these include Sweet, Joseph Wright and Napier from England, and Child, Kittredge and Cook from America. [59]

From the late nineteenth century onward, change and progress in the study of the living English language were decisively influenced and determined by the methods and principles of historical linguistics, particularly those of the Neogrammarians and their English and American contemporaries. This can be seen in lexicography (where further research on this specific question is needed), and above all in the grammatical description of English, which now, under the impact of historical grammar, is characterized by:

— a strictly descriptive approach: the grammarian records current usage and does not prescribe rules or issue prohibitions;

— (in some grammars, e.g., that of Jespersen) the historical explanation of Modern English, based on evidence from earlier stages of the language;

— the aim of precision and accuracy;

— the aim of completeness;

— (in some grammars) the inclusion of English phonetics;

— the detailed treatment of syntax, which now makes up most of the grammatical description.[33]

These are the characteristics of the large, comprehensive grammars of English which appeared approximately between 1890 and 1935, and which in turn influenced the many shorter, more practical grammar-books also published during this time and in later years. A worthy predecessor was Eduard Mätzner with his three-volume *Englische Grammatik* (1860–65); Henry Sweet still refers to Mätzner in the programmatic preface to his *A New English Grammar Logical and Historical* (1891–98). Three comprehensive descriptions of English followed somewhat later: Otto Jespersen, *A Modern English Grammar on Historical Principles* (1909–49), Etsko Kruisinga, *A Handbook of Present-Day English* (first published 1909–11), and Hendrik Poutsma, *A Grammar of Late Modern English* (1904–26). The series was concluded by *A Grammar of the English Language* (1931–35) of the American professor George O. Curme. After this there was a gap of almost forty years before a new, comprehensive English grammar appeared that marked genuine progress in method and presentation, the *Grammar of Contemporary English* by Randolph Quirk, Sidney Greenbaum, Geoffrey Leech and Jan Svartvik (1972).

If one takes a glance through the above list of names of early twentieth-century authors who wrote the great handbooks of Modern English, it becomes clear that most of them were not native speakers of English. One reason for this may have been that England only woke up late to the need to teach the new world language (both as a foreign language and, later, as

---

[33] Further research will need to clarify the extent to which nineteenth-century grammars of the living language before Mätzner and Sweet were an advance on the eighteenth-century manuals in terms of completeness and reliability. Among the best-known works of the period that aimed at a comprehensive treatment of English was the 1122-page book by Goold Brown, *The Grammar of English Grammars,* first published in 1850 at Boston, Mass.

a second language). Here, Henry Sweet is an early exception; apart from phonetics (for which see below), the work of the English pioneers in this field—A. S. Hornby, Harold Palmer and Michael West—was not begun until the 1920s.[34] It was only after the Second World War that this area of applied linguistics came to full fruition in England as a university discipline, in publications such as the journal *English Language Teaching* (from 1946), and in the 'learner dictionaries' with their special (but even now not wholly satisfactory) provisions for syntax and idioms; *An Advanced Learner's Dictionary of Current Idiomatic English* by Hornby, Gatenby and Wakefield (first published in 1948), and the *Dictionary of Contemporary English* by Paul Procter (1978) are the best-known representatives of this genre.

The system and the categories of linguistic description used in the great grammars mentioned above are on the whole 'traditional,' but an attempt at innovation was made by Jespersen with his categories of *rank, nexus* and *junction.* The shorter, one-volume English grammars also remained basically traditional for a long time, one of the reasons being the desire to preserve a uniform terminology for the teaching of both English and foreign languages. In England, this had been recommended in 1911 by Edward A. Sonnenschein (professor of classical philology at Birmingham from 1883) and the Joint Committee on Grammatical Terminology under his chairmanship; similar recommendations were made a little later by a corresponding American committee. [60]

Besides the grammars and dictionaries of Modern English, from the second half of the nineteenth century onward numerous language manuals, often with *Usage, Style* or *Composition* in their titles, were published in England and America. One of the first works of this type was Dean Henry Alford's *The Queen's English* (first edition 1863), a well-known but notoriously controversial book; however, the careful reader will find that it is far more liberal and realistic than some of its critics would make us believe. In content, these manuals considerably overlap with grammars, but they are more clearly normative in intention. Such practice—and the type of book—have met with a good deal of criticism, though again critics often fail to realize that, like the allegedly prescriptive grammars of the eighteenth century, these manuals were intended to serve a practical purpose, and it seems remarkable that in recent years lexicographers of Modern English

---

[34] On Hornby, Palmer and West, who gained much of their experience in teaching foreign languages in Japan and India, see the recent *The Oxford Companion to the English Language,* ed. Tom McArthur (Oxford, 1992).

have decided to make their books more helpful by including 'Usage notes,' thus in fact continuing what Dean Alford and the Fowler Brothers (*The King's English*, 1906; *Modern English Usage*, 1926) had begun. [61]

5. New Disciplines in Language Study

Up to the nineteenth century, the areas of interest for linguists, grammarians and lexicographers remained within more or less fixed bounds. But increasing specialization came with the new knowledge and methodology introduced by historical linguistics, a development which has continued to the present. New linguistic disciplines arose in the nineteenth century, yet a closer inspection soon reveals that they were by no means completely novel and original; it therefore seems preferable to speak of these disciplines not as coming into existence, but rather as becoming independent. Three of the earliest and most important will be considered here in the context of the descriptive and explanatory study of English: phonetics, semantics and dialectology, and the subjects closely related to dialectology, the study of names and the investigation of the varieties of English outside its mother country.

Phonetics

Phonetics reached a high point of its development in England in the late nineteenth century. It was mainly for three reasons that particular importance was attached to research into the phonetic system of English at that time:

1. A reform of English spelling, repeatedly called for, was only conceivable if it was carried out on a phonetic basis.
2. Historical linguists, and particularly the Neogrammarians, had found that language change and the phonology of the earlier periods of languages needed to be investigated with the aid of the living languages, in other words with the aid of the phonetics of these languages.
3. Phonetics had a key role to play in the teaching of modern languages—above all of English—and in the reform of teaching methods.

According to the *Oxford English Dictionary*, the term *phonetics* is first recorded in Robert Latham's *The English Language* (1841)—the adjective *phonetic* slightly earlier—but it had its predecessor since the seventeenth century in the term *orthoepy*. The promising beginnings of this discipline can be traced to the late sixteenth and especially the seventeenth century, while in the ancient and medieval periods phonetics tended to be neglected. Several reasons may account for such neglect: insufficient knowledge of human physiology; the treatment of sound and syllable especially in the context of metrics; probably also the fact that neither in Classical and Medieval Latin nor in Old and Middle English the relationship between sounds and letters had ever caused problems comparable to those posed by Modern English from the fifteenth century onwards. There were, however, some remarkable early attempts to describe the articulation of speech sounds, as in the third book of *De nuptiis Philologiae et Mercurii* of Martianus Capella, and in the *Tractatus de Grammatica* ascribed to Robert Grosseteste.[35]

The treatment of phonetics by sixteenth- and seventeenth-century English authors is characterized by the aim to describe and classify the speech sounds by means of the place and manner of their articulation. In addition, there were the efforts to introduce a reformed alphabet and spelling more suited to the sounds of the language, or a kind of phonetic transcription. This development has been outlined above and has been covered extensively in linguistic literature; here, however, it seems important to point to the context and aims of the early attempts at phonetic analysis. These are found not only within the circle of the spelling reformers—where, quite early, Sir Thomas Smith and John Hart distinguished themselves as phoneticians—but also among the grammarians who aimed at a description of English suitable also for the teaching of foreigners; foremost as phoneticians among this group were John Wallis and Christopher Cooper. Along with the 'general' phoneticians of the period, Robert Robinson (*The Art of Pronuntiation,* 1617) and William Holder (*Elements of Speech,* 1669), the latter group proceeded much more systematically than the spelling reformers and prepared the ground for a more general science of phonetics—already envisaged by John Hart, it seems, which could be applied to the analysis of all spoken languages. A fourth and final group of phoneticians in the seventeenth century, and one whose contribution should not be underestimated, included scholars such as Francis Lodwick and John Wilkins, who planned universal languages intended to be spoken

---

[35] See *Martianus Capella,* ed. James Willis (Leipzig, 1983), 68–69, iii.261; *Tractatus de Grammatica: Eine fälschlich Robert Grosseteste zugeschriebene spekulative Grammatik,* ed. Karl Reichl, Veröffentlichungen des Grabmann-Institutes, 28 (Munich, 1976).

as well as written. As a consequence, phonological systems had to be devised that were supposed to be equally universal in nature and application; their designers drew on English and other known languages, describing sounds according to articulatory criteria.[36]

Occupation with English pronunciation continued throughout the eighteenth century, but now the main emphasis was placed on the practical and normative pronouncing dictionaries discussed above. In one of these, *The Grand Repository of the English Language* (1775) by Thomas Spence, each word is even transcribed into a genuine phonetic script, but this book seems to have appeared in only one edition and has long since been forgotten.

It was only in the nineteenth century that a phonetics based on strictly scientific principles developed. In England the main concern, as ever, was the problem of a spelling reform. In 1837, Isaac Pitman published his new shorthand system on a phonetic basis. His interest in phonetics, coupled with his experiences as a teacher, led Pitman to devise a new, phonetic writing system for English, which he developed in cooperation with Alexander Ellis and which appeared as *Phonotype* in 1847. Ellis later went on experimenting with other notations on the basis of the roman alphabet and used one of them, his "Palaeotype," in his work *On Early English Pronunciation* (1869–89). Ellis's transcription systems had a far-reaching influence on later phoneticians, among them Henry Sweet. The same cannot exactly be said for the "Visible Speech" of Alexander Melville Bell, a teacher of elocution in London. His *Visible Speech, The Science of Universal Alphabetics, or Self-Interpreting Physiological Letters for the Printing and Writing of all Languages in one Alphabet* came out in 1867. An admirable but unfortunately impractical system, it represented every known or imaginable sound by a symbol whose individual elements indicated the precise manner of articulation of that sound. Despite its practical shortcomings, Bell's work contributed significantly to the later development of English phonetics.

The role and importance of phonetics in the study of language, and in particular of the English language, in the last quarter of the nineteenth century is well illustrated by several basic handbooks published in quick succession: Eduard Sievers, *Grundzüge der Lautphysiologie* (1876), with its telling subtitle *Zur Einführung in das Studium der Lautlehre der indogermanischen Sprachen* ("An Introduction to the Study of the Phonology of the

---

[36] Worthy of note is a phonetic, non-alphabetic script for the transcription of Algonkian designed by Thomas Harriot; see Vivian Salmon, "Thomas Harriot (1560–1621) and the English Origins of Algonkian Linguistics," *Historiographia Linguistica* 19 (1992): 25–56.

Indo-European Languages"); Henry Sweet, *A Handbook of Phonetics* (1877)—the most influential of these works, and the first of a whole series of writings on phonetics by Sweet (it led Sievers to revise his own book, particularly the section on vowels, published from 1881 as *Grundzüge der Phonetik*); Wilhelm Viëtor, *Elemente der Phonetik und Orthoepie des Deutschen, Englischen und Französischen* (1884); finally, and somewhat later, Otto Jespersen's *Lehrbuch der Phonetik* (1904). Their authors can also be considered as the founders of the phonetics of the modern languages. In 1886, Jespersen, Viëtor and Sweet were among the first to join "The Phonetic Teachers Association" founded by Paul Passy and renamed "International Phonetic Association" in 1897. It is to this association that we owe the creation of a phonetic alphabet on scientific principles that could be employed in transcribing not only English and the modern languages; its first version was published in 1888. Passy, it should be noted, was the teacher of Daniel Jones, who founded the London school of phonetics and devised the system of cardinal vowels; Jones's books decisively determined the development of English phonetics in the twentieth century.

As is well known, the phoneticians of the late nineteenth century were pioneers in linguistics and in language teaching methodology. Viëtor's *Der Sprachunterricht muss umkehren!* ("Language Teaching Must Start Afresh"), first published under the pseudonym "Quousque tandem" in 1882, has long been a classic of the genre.[37] Henry Sweet, who gained academic recognition in England only very late, towers above his contemporaries as a historical philologist, phonetician, grammarian, and also as an authority on methods of language learning. The phoneme, one of the key elements of modern phonology and structuralism, already exists as a concept (even if it is not named as such) behind Sweet's "Broad Romic" script, for which he gives the rule "that only those distinctions of sounds require to be symbolized in any one language which are *independently significant*" (*A Handbook of Phonetics*, p. 104; my italics). [62]

Semantics

The study of meaning became known in English from the 1890s, on the model of Michel Bréal's term, as *semantics*. Other, earlier expressions now

---

[37]An English translation of this influential pamphlet, by A. P. R. Howatt, David Abercrombie and Beat Buchmann, is now available, printed as Appendix to A. P. R. Howatt, *A History of English Language Teaching* (Oxford, 1984), 340–63.

no longer in use were *semasiology* (first recorded in 1847, probably after Christian Carl Reisig), and *sematology* (from 1880). While semantics may have been new as a linguistic discipline, the object of its study had been known for centuries. Questions of meaning, particularly the meaning of words, had been a perennial problem for translators and lexicographers. Samuel Johnson tackled the subject thoroughly and systematically in the preface to his *Dictionary,* where he deals with the "explanation" and the "progress of meaning" of words. Another related field was the study of synonyms, which is based on semantic definitions and distinctions. In this respect, Elizabeth Jane Whately showed particular perspicacity and sound method in her *Selection of English Synonyms* (first published in 1851). Also, the phenomenon of semantic change cannot be separated from the analysis of rhetorical tropes. The relations between word and object, concept and meaning, had already been treated by the English philosophers and linguists of the seventeenth century (Bacon, Hobbes, Locke; John Wilkins), and much earlier than that by the *modistae* and, again before them, by John of Salisbury in his *Metalogicon* (III.ii).

The largely historical interests of nineteenth-century linguists also determined the beginnings of semantics. Not surprisingly, then, attention focused on change of meaning; the aim was to achieve a clear idea of the processes involved in such change and, at the same time, to contribute to the methodical foundation of etymological research, for precise and reliable criteria were now available for the study of sound changes, whereas "human fancy . . . runs riot in the region of meaning," as John P. Postgate, classical philologist and professor of comparative philology at University College, London, noted in his inaugural address of 1896, in which he urged the establishment of a new "science of meaning."[38]

Several decades before, the way had been prepared for this new discipline in England by Richard Chenevix Trench, whose work has already been mentioned in connection with the *Oxford English Dictionary*. In his lectures and books, Trench discussed in great detail the history of words and semantic change in English, though without aiming at a strictly systematic treatment; he linked his linguistic observations to developments in cultural history, but also to religious convictions and moral judgments.

It took another few decades until systematic studies of semantic change

---

[38] Printed as Appendix, "The Science of Meaning," in Michel Bréal, *Semantics: Studies in the Science of Meaning,* trans. Mrs. Henry Cust (New York, 1900), 311–36.

in English appeared; the reasons for this delay must lie, at least partly, in
the lack of a historical dictionary to serve as a reliable basis for such work.
At any rate, it seems remarkable that the early pioneering studies in this
area were English translations of three works by continental scholars with
Neogrammarian backgrounds. These not only examine the phenomenon
of semantic change, but also the reasons for such change, the psychological
factors conditioning it, and the role of the context in which it takes place.
The three works are Arsène Darmesteter's *La vie des mots* (the English
version appeared in 1886, a year before the French original); Hermann
Paul's *Prinzipien der Sprachgeschichte* (1889, translated into English from the
second German edition of 1886, with its new chapter on semantic
change);[39] and finally Michel Bréal's *Essai de sémantique* (1897, English
translation 1900). The same period also saw the publication of the first
volumes of the *Oxford English Dictionary,* and it is obvious that the earliest
scholarly studies of semantic change in English not only depended on the
methodical framework established in the continental works but also on the
materials now available in the new historical *Dictionary.* Thus James B.
Greenough and George L. Kittredge, professors at Harvard University,
expressly mention the *Dictionary* as one of the sources for their *Words and
their Ways in English Speech* (1902), a study of English lexicology in which
especially chapters xvi–xxii are devoted to semantic change. Henry Bradley, himself one of the editors of the *Oxford English Dictionary,* assigns
nearly a quarter of his *The Making of English* (1904) to the topic. These two
books, which incidentally were both aimed at a wider reading audience,
have retained their value as works of scholarship to the present day. Their
authors make clear the complexity of semantic processes and the impossi-
bility of assigning them to a system of clear-cut categories; they consider
context, connotation (including what Bradley calls "emotional connotation"), synonyms and homophones; they examine the phenomena as well
as their causes. Bradley not only observes change of meaning in the
context of a group of synonyms (or what was later called a 'semantic field'),
he also explicitly refers to "the common features" (p. 177) of the several
things denoted by the same word. [63]

---

[39] An adaptation of Paul's book in English, by H. A. Strong, W. S. Logeman and B.
I. Wheeler, appeared in 1891 under the title *Introduction to the Study of the History of
Language.*

The Study of Dialects and Names

In the field of dialect study, the last few decades have seen the completion and publication of excellent dialect atlases for England, Scotland, and for parts of the United States of America. Behind this achievement is a long development which goes back to the awareness of dialect differences in medieval England. As early as the Anglo-Saxon period, texts were transcribed from one dialect into another; differences between the Middle English dialects were already noted by several authors, from William of Malmesbury to William Caxton; dialect speech was used for literary effect, as in Chaucer's *Reeve's Tale* and in the *Wakefield Plays*.

With the antiquarian interest in the English language that began in the sixteenth century, there also developed an interest in the living dialects of English which found expression in a large number of publications of various sorts until well into the nineteenth century. Frequently, however, views and remarks concerning English dialects in this period were prescriptive in nature, for a new standard language had now evolved, which, according to Richard Puttenham in *The Arte of English Poesie* (1589), III.iv, was best represented by "the usual speach of the Court, and that of London and the shires lying about London within lx myles, and not much above." Prescriptive notes and warnings of this kind occur for example in Alexander Gill's *Logonomia Anglica,* where in the sixth chapter Gill makes the first attempt at a systematic description of the major English dialect areas, based mostly on phonetic criteria. References to dialects can be found in the work of the seventeenth- and eighteenth-century grammarians and rhetoricians, who comment on dialect pronunciation, including that of Cockney. Dialect poetry and glossaries of individual dialects also occur; besides these, we should not forget some of the early dictionaries which include dialect vocabulary, such as those by Coles, Kersey and Bailey, as well as Skinner's etymological dictionary. The first genuine dialect dictionary, John Ray's *A Collection of Words not Generally Used* (first edition 1674) has already been mentioned. Remarkably in advance of his time was Laurence Nowell with his Old English dictionary, compiled about 1565: whenever an Old English word no longer existed in the standard language of the sixteenth century, he supplied, if possible, its equivalent from contemporary dialects, particularly that of his home county, Lancashire.[40]

---

[40] Nowell's dictionary remained unprinted until it was edited by Albert H. Marckwardt, *Laurence Nowell's Vocabularium Saxonicum* (Ann Arbor, 1952).

Until the nineteenth century the study of dialects had more or less remained the province of amateurs, but from the time when dialect students were able to draw on the insights and methods of historical philology, it became a linguistic research discipline. Historical philology had brought a new understanding of dialects and of their value for the linguist—no longer were they viewed as second-rate or inferior. As a consequence, scholars were faced with the task of producing adequate descriptions of the living (and also of the historical) dialects of English, a task now made feasible through the advances in phonetics. In 1873, Walter William Skeat founded the English Dialect Society, which first and foremost was to compile a dialect dictionary. In 1882, Alexander J. Ellis reported very favorably to the Philological Society on Georg Wenker's *Sprachatlas des Deutschen Reiches,* although he found its treatment of phonetics not wholly satisfactory. Seven years later, Ellis published part V of his work *On Early English Pronunciation.* This volume, subtitled *The Existing Phonology of English Dialects Compared with that of West Saxon Speech,* was the first full study and inventory of (British) English dialects. Whereas earlier investigators had mainly examined and recorded dialect vocabulary, Ellis worked on a phonetic basis, and by means of isoglosses (including his ten 'Transverse Lines,' horizontally drawn across the country) he divided the English-speaking area into six 'divisions' and 42 'districts'. Although Ellis's book shows some methodical deficiencies and has now been superseded, it represents one of the pioneer works in English philology; any serious study of dialects was from now on inconceivable without their precise phonetic analysis.

In 1892 there appeared the first systematic description of a local English dialect, *A Grammar of the Dialect of Windhill in the West Riding of Yorkshire,* by Joseph Wright (1891 deputy professor of comparative philology at the University of Oxford, 1901 Max Müller's successor on the chair of Comparative Philology). This was followed by Wright's principal work, the *English Dialect Dictionary* (1896–1905), and his *English Dialect Grammar* (1905). For his *Dictionary*—which also covered Wales, Scotland and Ireland—Wright used already existing dialect glossaries and other printed sources as well as the findings from a questionnaire which he had sent out to 12,000 recipients. The result was a dictionary, which, while not being perfect, has remained indispensable, particularly as the editors of the *Oxford English Dictionary* (see their Introduction, I.xxviii) could not possibly record the full dialect vocabulary of Modern English. Wright's achievement is all the more remarkable in view of his educational background (largely that of a self-taught young worker) and his early career up to his attending university at Heidelberg and Leipzig.[41]

Work on English dialects was continued in the twentieth century by such scholars as Alois Brandl and his students at Berlin. But decisive progress was not made until after the Second World War with the *Survey of English Dialects* (with a historical orientation, and justifiably so) by Eugen Dieth and Harold Orton, and the *Linguistic Survey of Scotland,* with the resulting dialect atlases. The methodically pioneering *Linguistic Atlas of Late Medieval England* also belongs to this period. [64]

Closely related to dialect research is the study of names, the investigation of both place-names (including the names of fields, rivers, and streets) and personal names, which can yield valuable information on the historical development of settlements, on cultural history in general, and on the history of the language and its dialects. Naturally, the early antiquarians were interested in names; Camden in his *Remaines* (1605), Verstegan in his *Restitution* (1605), and Skinner in the "Etymologicon onomasticon," which formed part of his etymological dictionary of 1671, all sought to explain the names of English towns, villages and rivers, as well as Christian names and surnames. Camden's chapter on personal names in particular was still being used in the nineteenth century, since it had not been replaced by more recent work.

In putting the study of names on a sound scientific basis, historical linguistics again played a decisive role. Not surprisingly, the etymologies which the antiquarians found for names were often erroneous and not based on reliable evidence. A sound knowledge of historical phonology, and the collecting and dating of all early occurrences and forms of a name

---

[41] In a period where it is considered normal to claim one's right to an education, it is worth casting a glance at the educational careers of some of the leading English philologists at the turn of the century. James Murray (1837–1915), the first editor of the *Oxford English Dictionary,* attended school only to the age of fifteen and never went to university. Similarly, his successor, Henry Bradley (1846–1923), never enjoyed a university education, leaving school at the age of fourteen to work for four years as a private teacher and a further twenty years as an office clerk. Joseph Wright (1855–1930) started work in a textile factory at the age of seven; it was only at the age of fifteen that he taught himself to read and write. See K. M. Elisabeth Murray, *Caught in the Web of Words: James A. H. Murray and the Oxford English Dictionary* (New Haven, 1977); Robert Bridges, "Henry Bradley: A Memoir," in *The Collected Papers* by Henry Bradley (Oxford, 1928), 3–56; Elizabeth Mary Wright, *The Life of Joseph Wright,* 2 vols. (London, 1932). Even those scholars with university degrees had not been trained as 'English philologists'; see the autobiographical introduction to Walter W. Skeat, *A Student's Pastime* (Oxford, 1896), pp. vii–lxxviii, and C. L. Wrenn, "Henry Sweet," *Transactions of the Philological Society* (1946): 177–201.

now became the methodical prerequisites for all further work in the field. It was again Walter William Skeat who paved the way for place-name research with his book *The Place-Names of Cambridgeshire* (1901); a few other counties were covered in monographs in the next two decades, before in 1923 the English Place-Name Society took up its work. Since then, volumes for the individual counties have been published in regular succession by the Society, each arranged topographically and based on broad documentary evidence. Personal names, too, became the subject of analysis on philological principles from the later nineteenth century, notably in the posthumously published *Dictionary of English and Welsh Surnames* (1901) by Canon C. W. Bardsley, while *A History of Christian Names* by Charlotte M. Yonge (1863, revised 1884) remained unsatisfactory from an etymological point of view. A development similar to that in place-name studies then began in the twentieth century, with intensive research into the history of personal names, including those of the Old and Middle English periods. Scandinavian scholars, the foremost being Eilert Ekwall, have made outstanding contributions to the study of English names. [65]

English as a World Language and its Varieties

Richard Mulcaster at the end of the sixteenth century, and Jonathan Swift at the beginning of the eighteenth century (in his *Proposal for Correcting, Improving and Ascertaining the English Tongue*), are among those writers who noted that outside the British Isles, no one, or hardly any one, understood, read or learned English. By the middle of the eighteenth century, however, Lord Chesterfield could already speak of "the rapid progress which our language has lately made, and still continues to make, all over Europe."[42] In the course of the nineteenth century, English was increasingly recognized as a world language, and in the twentieth century it has become *the* world language; its present status will probably prevent the adoption and spread of an invented, artificial language such as Esperanto as a general *lingua franca*. [66] This development was already being observed by the middle of the nineteenth century. In February 1850, the librarian Thomas Watts read a paper to the Philological Society on the topic; less than a year later, in January 1851, Jacob Grimm gave a lecture

---

[42] Cited from Susie I. Tucker, *English Examined: Two Centuries of Comment on the Mother Tongue* (Cambridge, 1961), 91.

to the Berlin Academy "Über den Ursprung der Sprache" ("On the Origin of Language"), in which he emphasized the structural characteristics and the expressive power of the English language:

> Keine unter allen neueren sprachen hat gerade durch das aufgeben und zerrütten alter lautgesetze, durch den wegfall beinahe sämtlicher flexionen eine gröszere kraft und stärke empfangen als die englische und von ihrer nicht einmal lehrbaren, nur lernbaren fülle freier mitteltöne ist eine wesentliche gewalt des ausdrucks abhängig geworden, wie sie vielleicht noch nie einer andern menschlichen zunge zu gebote stand. ihre ganze überaus geistige, wunderbar geglückte anlage und durchbildung war hervorgegangen aus einer überraschenden vermählung der beiden edelsten sprachen des späteren Europas, der germanischen und romanischen, und bekannt ist wie im englischen sich beide zueinander verhalten, indem jene bei weitem die sinnliche grundlage hergab, diese die geistigen begriffe zuführte. ja die englische sprache, von der nicht umsonst auch der gröszte und überlegenste dichter der neuen zeit im gegensatz zur classischen alten poesie, ich kann natürlich nur Shakespeare meinen, gezeugt und getragen worden ist, sie darf mit vollem recht eine weltsprache heiszen und scheint gleich dem englischen volk ausersehn künftig noch in höherem masze an allen enden der erde zu walten. denn an reichthum, vernunft und gedrängter fuge läszt sich keine aller noch lebenden sprachen ihr an die seite setzen, auch unsre deutsche nicht, die zerrissen ist wie wir selbst zerrissen sind, und erst manche gebrechen von sich abschütteln müste ehe sie kühn mit in die laufbahn träte.[43]

---

[43] Jacob Grimm, *Kleinere Schriften,* vol.1: *Reden und Abhandlungen* (Berlin, 1864), p. 293. All of this passage was translated by S. H. in *Notes and Queries,* 7 (Feb. 5, 1853), 125–26, and, perhaps based on S. H., the latter part was given an improved rendering by Richard Chenevix Trench in *English Past and Present* (ed. Everyman's Library, 1927 and repr.), pp. 28–29:

> [S. H.:] "Of all modern languages, not one has acquired such great strength and vigour as the English. It has accomplished this by simply freeing itself from the ancient phonetic laws, and casting off almost all inflections; whilst, from its abundance of intermediate sounds, tones not even to be taught, but only to be learned, it has derived" [Trench:] "a veritable power of expression, such as perhaps never stood at the command of any other language of men. Its highly spiritual genius, and wonderfully happy development and condition, have been the result of a surprisingly intimate union of the two noblest languages in

The role of world language which English came to play was due not only to its status as an acquired second language but also to its spread as a mother tongue outside the British Isles and its use as a *lingua franca* in countries ruled by the British. The result was the development of what are now called 'varieties' of English, such as American English, Australian English, etc. As we see it now, philologists should have studied these, just as they studied the British dialects, but (ignoring American English for the moment) the first thorough treatments of those varieties do not appear until very late, in most cases not until the second half of this century. This is true even of the work by scholars who were themselves speakers of such varieties. In Arthur G. Kennedy's bibliography of the English language up to the year 1922, only 28 of a total of more than 13,000 entries are listed under the heading "Colonial English." Of these, about one third is concerned with English in Canada, in India and in Australia respectively; they include the most important and, for practical purposes, the most necessary works in this area, namely three dictionaries: of Anglo-Indian (Henry Yule and A. C. Burnell, *Hobson-Jobson, being a Glossary of Anglo-Indian Colloquial Words and Phrases,* first published in 1886), of Australian English (Edward E. Morris, *Austral English,* 1898), and of South African English (Charles Pettman, *Africanderisms,* 1913).

The reasons for the long neglect of overseas English are complex, but normative views may well have played a decisive role, as also the dominant interest in the historical study of the language. A remarkable exception was *Kultur und Sprache im neuen England* by Heinrich Spies, a book on the living English language first published in 1925, which dealt with such varieties as well as Pidgin English (and, moreover, what it called the "Negro English" of the United States).

---

modern Europe, the Teutonic and the Romance. It is well known in what relation these two stand to one another in the English tongue; the former supplying in far larger proportion the material groundwork, the latter the spiritual conceptions. In truth the English language, which by no mere accident has produced and upborne the greatest and most predominant poet of modern times, as distinguished from the ancient classical poetry (I can, of course, only mean Shakespeare), may with all right be called a world-language; and, like the English people, appears destined hereafter to prevail with a sway more extensive even than its present over all the portions of the globe. For in wealth, good sense, and closeness of structure no other of the languages at this day spoken deserves to be compared with it—not even our German, which is torn, even as we are torn, and must first rid itself of many defects, before it can enter boldly into the lists as a competitor with the English."

Although the English-based pidgins and creoles of Africa, the Pacific and the Caribbean can provide instructive insights into the processes of language contact and linguistic change, scholars have only recently directed their attention to these languages. Far in advance of his time was the work of Hugo Schuchardt, professor at Graz, who began work on such languages as early as 1871, though on the basis of written documents only; his "Kreolische Studien" appeared from 1882 onwards. What until then had been mainly the province of missionaries became through Schuchardt, and later through Otto Jespersen (in chapter xii of his *Language: Its Nature, Development and Origin,* 1922), the object of linguistic analysis. [67]

American English

Of all the varieties of English outside the British Isles, American English became the most important already in the course of the nineteenth century. Nevertheless, final recognition and thorough scholarly treatment was a long time in coming. As late as 1925, at the beginning of his book *The English Language in America,* George Philip Krapp remarked: "Though American histories of other kinds abound, of politics, of diplomacy, of painting, music, even of furniture, the American language has strangely escaped historical treatment." The reasons for this almost certainly lay in the normative views of language in the eighteenth and nineteenth centuries, and in the long-lasting prejudice that only the English spoken and written in Britain could provide a linguistic standard; in this, political convictions may also have played a role.

By the eighteenth century, American English had already acquired characteristics which clearly distinguished it from British English and which until well into the twentieth century have been the reason for negative comments against it. What proved particularly harmful to its status was the fact that such negative judgments came not only from the British, as was to be expected, but also from the Americans themselves. This begins with John Witherspoon, a Scottish clergyman, who came to America in 1769 on his appointment as president of the College of New Jersey (since 1896 Princeton University); later, as a member of the Continental Congress, he became a dedicated supporter of American independence. Witherspoon set forth his criticism of American English in a series of articles published in journals in Philadelphia in 1781, where he is the first to employ the term *Americanism.* His basic view, however, was that the development of an American variety of English was perfectly natural and therefore not to be considered a drawback. Much sharper criticism came from the pen of the American lawyer and philologist John Pickering, to whom we owe the first dictionary of Americanisms (*A Vocabulary or collection of words and phrases which have been supposed to be peculiar to the United States of America,* 1816). This prejudiced attitude continued for a long time and is even found with literary authors and competent linguists. It was only from the middle of the nineteenth century that American literary figures like James Russell Lowell and Mark Twain turned away from the strict observation of British English usage. Even towards the end of the century, some North American philologists show remarkable reserve when dealing with their own language in accounts of the history of English. In Oliver F. Emerson's *History of the English Language* (1894) a mere six pages are devoted to American English, although the same author was responsible for the first scholarly investigation of an American dialect (*The Ithaca Dialect: A Study of Present English,* 1891). In Thomas R. Lounsbury's *History of the English Language* (1879; second edition 1894), American English is completely ignored. As late as 1963, Raven I. McDavid, one of the great authorities in the field, complained of the lack of attention paid to American English in research programs at universities in the USA.[44]

In the face of negative criticism, scholars soon rose up to defend their native tongue. Their views were motivated by a national pride that went back to the days of the Declaration of Independence, but they were also determined by a clear-sighted regard for linguistic realities. The first of them, and the most important and influential, was Noah Webster (1758–1843), a lawyer and teacher, whose *Dissertations on the English Language* (1789) called for a spelling reform and emphasized the independence of American English: "As an independent nation, our honor requires us to have a system of our own, in language as well as government," and ". . . several circumstances render a future separation of the American Tongue from the English, necessary and unavoidable" (*Dissertations,* pp. 20 and 22). Webster put his thoughts into practice in his dictionaries, which in their entries took account of American usage: *A Compendious Dictionary of the English Language* (1806), and *An American Dictionary of the English Language* (1828). Besides his *American Spelling Book* (first issued in 1783 as part I of *A Grammatical Institute of the English Language*), his *American Dictionary* (frequently printed and revised in the nineteenth century) became for a

---

[44] Raven I. McDavid, Jr., "American English: A Bibliographic Essay," *American Studies International* 17,2 (1979): 3–45, especially p. 7.

considerable time the most influential book on language in America and might have held a monopoly almost to the end of the century, were it not for the appearance of a serious rival: in 1830, Joseph Worcester, apparently a former collaborator of Webster, began publishing his own dictionaries (which in orthography and usage were more conservative than those by Webster) and thus instigated the frequently cited "war of the dictionaries." [68]

After the introduction of historical linguistics as an academic discipline at American universities, American English became the subject of genuine interest and serious research. Oliver F. Emerson, Charles Hall Grandgent and George Hempl were among the early and leading scholars in the field. The founding of the American Dialect Society at Harvard University in 1889, with Francis James Child as its first president, marked a decisive step forward. Nevertheless, another thirty years were to pass before the publication of the first comprehensive treatment of American English. In 1919 Henry Louis Mencken's pioneering work was published under the programmatic title *The American Language*. Written by a journalist rather than a philologist, it gave extensive consideration to colloquial usage. Apart from a few dictionaries of Americanisms (after Pickering the first was John Russell Bartlett's *Glossary of Words and Phrases Usually Regarded as Peculiar to the United States,* 1848), it was only in the decades after the publication of Mencken's classic work that the great handbooks and reference works of American English appeared: G. P. Krapp's *The English Language in America* (see above), the *Dictionary of American English on Historical Principles* by Sir William Craigie and James Hulbert (1938–44), and the dialect atlases; the journal *American Speech* was founded in 1925. [69]

6. The Twentieth Century: A Note

As I remarked in the Introduction, this brief historical survey cannot deal with the many and varied, often enough rapid and even revolutionary developments in English language scholarship in the course of the twentieth century. But as the foregoing sections will have shown, there is no absolute dividing line between the nineteenth century and the twentieth, just as there is no such fixed borderline between the seventeenth and eighteenth centuries. While the first half of this century is largely characterized by the continuation of what was achieved or begun in the nineteenth century, the second half, though well aware of traditions and continuities, is increasingly breaking out into new territory, where we encounter new grammatical models and new methods in lexicography or dialect research as well as new or newly developing, often highly specialized linguistic disciplines. No doubt an important factor here is the role of technology, particularly the possibilities offered by sound recording and data-processing. It is to be hoped that from these new developments and possibilities, English language scholarship—descriptive and historical—will draw further impetus, support and profit in the years to come and in the more distant future. [70]

PART II: BIBLIOGRAPHY

Introductory note

English language scholarship as far as it is printed has been fully record-ed, with only few omissions, for the time up to and including 1922 in Arthur G. Kennedy's monumental *Bibliography of Writings on the English Language*. No such bibliography exists for the seventy years from 1923 until the present. What follows here is intended as a bibliographical guide to the fields covered in Part I of this book, and as a substitute for bulky footnotes. It should be emphasized, however, that this is a select bibliography, with all the imperfections (and, I hope, advantages) that such a compilation necessarily has. I have tried to select comprehensive treatments of the various subjects as well as other important and useful publications, especial-ly such as are representative of the state of present-day scholarship. Titles published up to the end of 1993 have been included, but only very few that have appeared in 1994 or early in 1995. The Bibliography is in gener-al restricted to books and articles *about* the study of English; the primary literature has been exhaustively listed in the works of Kennedy and Alston. Frequently cited publications will be found with full details in the list of abbreviations and abbreviated titles; references to them are always marked by an asterisk. Cross-references within the Bibliography (in cases where one and the same title is listed in more than one section) are in square brackets; the numbers given in these brackets refer to section and item number of the Bibliography.

Abbreviations and abbreviated titles

Aarsleff (1967)★   Aarsleff, Hans, *The Study of Language in England: 1780–1860* (Princeton, N. J., 1967). [The 'second edition' (Minneapolis, 1983) is a reprint with an additional Preface, pp. v–xiii.]

Aarsleff *et al.* (1987)★   Aarsleff, Hans, Louis G. Kelly and Hans-Josef Niederehe, eds, *Papers in the History of Linguistics: Proceedings of the Third International Conference on the History of the Language Sciences (ICHoLS III), Princeton, 19–23 August 1984,* SHLS, 38 (Amsterdam, 1987).

Alston★   Alston, R. C., *A Bibliography of the English Language from the Invention of Printing to the Year 1800,* 11 vols and a supplement to vols I–X (Leeds, Bradford and Ilkley, 1965–1977). [Another edition, reproduced from the author's personal copy, with corrections and indices to vols I–X, was published in 1974 by Janus Press, Ilkley. Cf. Donald Gutch, *HL,* 2 (1975), 233–8.]

Archiv   *Archiv für das Studium der neueren Sprachen und Literaturen*

Arens (1969)★   Arens, Hans, *Sprachwissenschaft: Der Gang ihrer Entwicklung von der Antike bis zur Gegenwart,* sec. ed. (Freiburg, 1969).

ASE   *Anglo-Saxon England*

Baugh-Cable★   Baugh, Albert C., *A History of the English Language,* fourth ed. rev. Thomas Cable (Englewood Cliffs, N. J., 1993).

Beyer★   Beyer, Arno, *Deutsche Einflüsse auf die englische Sprachwissenschaft im 19. Jahrhundert,* Göppinger Arbeiten zur Germanistik, 324 (Stuttgart, 1981).

Brinkmann★   Brinkmann, Hennig, *Mittelalterliche Hermeneutik* (Tübingen, 1980).

Bynon-Palmer★   Bynon, Theodora and F. R. Palmer, eds, *Studies in the History of Western Linguistics: In Honour of R. H. Robins* (Cambridge, 1986).

CC   Corpus Christianorum

ES	*English Studies*
Gneuss (1990)★	Gneuss, Helmut, "The Study of Language in Anglo-Saxon England," *Bulletin of the John Rylands University Library of Manchester,* 72 (1990), 3–32.
Hartmann (1986)★	Hartmann, R. R. K., ed., *The History of Lexicography: Papers from the Dictionary Research Centre Seminar at Exeter, March 1986,* SHLS, 40 (Amsterdam, 1986).
HL	*Historiographia Linguistica. International Journal for the History of Linguistics*
Howatt★	Howatt, A. P. R., *A History of English Language Teaching* (Oxford, 1984).
T. Hunt★	Hunt, Tony, *Teaching and Learning Latin in Thirteenth-Century England,* 3 vols (Cambridge, 1991).
ICHoLS	International Conference on the History of the Language Sciences
JEGP	*Journal of English and Germanic Philology*
JL	Janua Linguarum
Jones (1953)★	Jones, Richard Foster, *The Triumph of the English Language: A Survey of Opinions Concerning the Vernacular from the Introduction of Printing to the Restoration* (Stanford, Calif., 1953).
Kennedy★	Kennedy, Arthur G., *A Bibliography of Writings on the English Language from the Beginning of Printing to the End of 1922* (Cambridge, Mass., 1927; repr. New York, 1961). [Supplemented by Arvid Gabrielson, *Studia Neophilologica,* 2 (1929), 117–68, Hermann M. Flasdieck, *Anglia Beiblatt,* 39 (1928), 166–74, and Rudolf Brotanek, *ZAA,* 4 (1956), 5–18.]
Leitner(1986)★	Leitner, Gerhard, ed., *The English Reference Grammar: Language and Linguistics, Writers and Readers,* Linguistische Arbeiten, 172 (Tübingen, 1986).
Leitner (1991)★	Leitner, Gerhard, ed., *English Traditional Grammars. An International Perspective,* SHLS, 62 (Amsterdam, 1991).
McKnight★	McKnight, George H., *The Evolution of the English Language: From Chaucer to the Twentieth Century* (New York, 1956; reprinted from the original edition of 1928, which was entitled *Modern English in the Making*).
Manitius★	Manitius, Max, *Geschichte der lateinischen Literatur des Mittelalters,* 3 vols (Munich, 1911–1931).

Mencken-McDavid★   Mencken, H. L., *The American Language: An Inquiry into the Development of English in the United States,* fourth ed. and two supplements abridged by Raven I. McDavid, Jr (New York, 1963).

Michael (1970)★   Michael, Ian, *English Grammatical Categories and the Tradition to 1800* (Cambridge, 1970).

Nagashima★   Nagashima, Daisuke, *Johnson the Philologist,* The Intercultural Research Institute Monograph, 20 (Hirakata, 1988).

NM   *Neuphilologische Mitteilungen*

Padley (1976)★, (1985)★, (1988)★   Padley, G. A., *Grammatical Theory in Western Europe 1500–1700,* 3 vols (Cambridge, 1976–1988); [I:] *The Latin Tradition* (1976), [II:] *Trends in Vernacular Grammar I* (1985), [III:] *Trends in Vernacular Grammar II* (1988).

Parret★   Parret, Herman, ed., *History of Linguistic Thought and Contemporary Linguistics* (Berlin, 1976).

PMLA   *Publications of the Modern Language Association of America*

RE★   *Paulys Realencyclopädie der Classischen Altertumswissenschaft,* rev. Georg Wissowa, ed. Konrat Ziegler *et al.,* Reihe 1: 24 vols, Reihe 2: 10 vols [= 68 Halbbände], 15 supplementary vols (Stuttgart, 1894–1976).

Robins (1990)★   Robins, R. H., *A Short History of Linguistics,* third ed. (London, 1990).

Sebeok (1975)★   Sebeok, Thomas A. *et al.,* eds, *Current Trends in Linguistics,* 14 vols in 21 (The Hague, 1963–1976), vol. XIII: *Historiography of Linguistics,* in 2 vols (1975).

SHLS   Studies in the History of the Language Sciences (Amsterdam Studies in the Theory and History of Linguistic Science, III)

SP   *Studies in Philology*

Starnes (1954)★   Starnes, DeWitt T., *Renaissance Dictionaries: English-Latin and Latin-English* (Austin, Texas, 1954).

Starnes-Noyes★   Starnes, DeWitt T. and Gertrude E. Noyes, *The English Dictionary from Cawdrey to Johnson 1604–1755,* new edition with introduction and select bibliography by Gabriele Stein, SHLS, 57 (Amsterdam, 1991). [Original ed. Chapel Hill, N. C., 1946]

Stein (1985)★   Stein, Gabriele, *The English Dictionary before Cawdrey,* Lexicographica, Series Maior, 9 (Tübingen, 1985).

TPS	*Transactions of the Philological Society*
TüBL	Tübinger Beiträge zur Linguistik
TUEPh	Münchener Universitäts-Schriften, Philosophische Fakultät, Texte und Untersuchungen zur Englischen Philologie
WDD*	Hausmann, Franz Josef, Oskar Reichmann, Herbert Ernst Wiegand and Ladislav Zgusta, eds, *Wörterbücher—Dictionaries—Dictionnaires: An International Encyclopedia of Lexicography*, 3 vols (Berlin, 1989–1991).
ZAA	*Zeitschrift für Anglistik und Amerikanistik*

1. Bibliographies

1. Arens (1969)★, pp. 753–98.
2. Koerner, E. F. K., *Western Histories of Linguistic Thought: An Annotated Chronological Bibliography 1822–1976*, SHLS, 11 (Amsterdam, 1978).
3. Salus, Peter H., *Panini to Postal: A Bibliography in the History of Linguistics*, Linguistic Bibliography Series, 2 (Edmonton, Alberta, 1971).
4. Stankiewicz, Edward, "Bibliography of the History of Linguistics," in Sebeok (1975)★, pp. 1381–446.
5. Alston★
6. Kennedy★
7. Reichl, Karl, *Englische Sprachwissenschaft. Eine Bibliographie*. Mit einem Anhang von Helmut Gneuss (Berlin, 1993).
   See also the relevant sections in annual bibliographies, esp.:
8. *Bibliographie linguistique de l'année 19–*, 1– (1949 [for 1939–1947]–).
9. *Bibliographie unselbständiger Literatur. Linguistik*, ed. Elke Suchan *et al.*, vols 1–3 (for 1971–1975); vol. 4– (for 1978–) under the title *Bibliographie linguistischer Literatur: Bibliographie zur allgemeinen Linguistik und zur anglistischen, germanistischen und romanistischen Linguistik*.
10. *MLA International Bibliography of Books and Articles on the Modern Languages and Literatures*. [Separately published since 1969; previously (for 1921–1967) as part of the *Publications of the Modern Language Association of America*. Bibliographies for 1921–1955 cover only American scholarship; bibliographies from that for 1968 onwards include a section "History of linguistics".]
11. *The Year's Work in English Studies*, 49– (for 1968–).

2. Periodicals and serial publications

1. *Beiträge zur Geschichte der Sprachwissenschaft*, 1– (1991–).
2. *Histoire, Épistémologie, Langage*, 1– (1979–).
3. *HL*, 1– (1974–).
4. *The Henry Sweet Society Newsletter*, 1– (1984–).
5. SHLS, 1– (1973–).
   Nos 3 and 4 include "Publications received" and reviews.

3. Theory and method of the historiography of linguistics

1. Arens, Hans, "Zur neueren Geschichtsschreibung der Linguistik," *HL*, 4 (1977), 319–82.
2. Brekle, Herbert Ernst, *Einführung in die Geschichte der Sprachwissenschaft* (Darmstadt, 1985).
3. Grotsch, Klaus, *Sprachwissenschaftsgeschichtsschreibung: Ein Beitrag zur Kritik und zur historischen und methodologischen Selbstvergewisserung der Disziplin,* Göppinger Arbeiten zur Germanistik, 325 (Göppingen, 1982).
4. Koerner, E. F. K., *Toward a Historiography of Linguistics: Selected Essays,* SHLS, 19 (Amsterdam, 1978).
5. Malkiel, Yakov and Margaret H. Langdon, "History and Histories of Linguistics," *Romance Philology,* 22 (1969), 530–74.
6. Schmitter, Peter, *Untersuchungen zur Historiographie der Linguistik: Struktur—Methodik—theoretische Fundierung,* TüBL, 181 (Tübingen, 1982).
7. Schmitter, Peter, ed., *Zur Theorie und Methode der Geschichtsschreibung der Linguistik,* Geschichte der Sprachtheorie, Analysen und Reflexionen, 1 (Tübingen, 1987).
8. Swiggers, Pierre, "La méthodologie de l'historiographie de la linguistique," *Folia Linguistica Historica,* 4 (1983), 55–79.

4. Histories of linguistics

1. Sebeok (1975)★
2. Arens (1969)★
3. Robins (1990)★
4. Amirova, T. A., B. A. Ol'chovikov and Ju. V. Roždestvenskij, *Abriss der Geschichte der Linguistik,* trans. Barbara Meier, ed. Georg Friedrich Meier (Leipzig, 1980). [Original ed. in Russian, 1975]
5. Arens, Hans, "Geschichte der Linguistik," in *Lexikon der germanistischen Linguistik,* ed. Peter Althaus, Helmut Henne and Herbert Ernst Wiegand, sec. ed., 4 vols (Tübingen, 1980), I, 97–107.
6. Berésin, F. M., *Geschichte der sprachwissenschaftlichen Theorien,* trans. and ed. Hans Zikmund (Leipzig, 1980).
7. Dinneen, Francis Patrick, *An Introduction to General Linguistics* (New York, 1967).
8. Harris, Roy and Talbot J. Taylor, *Landmarks in Linguistic Thought: The*

Western Tradition from Socrates to Saussure (London, 1989).

9. Itkonen, Esa, *Universal History of Linguistics: India, China, Arabia, Europe,* SHLS, 65 (Amsterdam, 1991).

10. Ivić, Milka, *Trends in Linguistics,* trans. Muriel Heppel, JL, Series Minor, 42 (The Hague, 1965). [Original ed. in Serbo-Croatian, 1963]

11. Lepschy, Giulio C., ed., *History of Linguistics.* Vol. I: *The Eastern Traditions of Linguistics;* Vol. II: *Classical and Medieval Linguistics* (London, 1994).

12. Mounin, Georges, *Histoire de la linguistique des origines au XXᵉ siècle* (Paris, 1967).

13. Robins, R. H., *Ideen- und Problemgeschichte der Sprachwissenschaft: Mit besonderer Berücksichtigung des 19. und 20. Jahrhunderts,* trans. C. Gutknecht and K.-U. Panther, Schwerpunkte Linguistik und Kommunikationswissenschaft, 16 (Frankfurt/Main, 1973).

14. Thomsen, Vilhelm, *Geschichte der Sprachwissenschaft bis zum Ausgang des 19. Jahrhunderts: Kurzgefasste Darstellung der Hauptpunkte,* trans. Hans Pollak (Halle, 1927).

15. Waterman, John T., *Perspectives in Linguistics* (Chicago, 1963).

16. Law, Vivien, "Language and its Students: the History of Linguistics," in *An Encyclopaedia of Language,* ed. N. E. Collinge (London, 1990), pp. 784–842.

4a. Collections of essays and papers

1. Koerner, Konrad, ed., *Progress in Linguistic Historiography: Papers from the First International Conference on the History of the Language Sciences (Ottawa, 28–31 August 1978),* SHLS, 20 (Amsterdam, 1980).

2. Auroux, Sylvain, Michel Glatigny, André Joly, Anne Nicolas and Irène Rosier, eds, *Matériaux pour une histoire des théories linguistiques* [ICHoLS II, Lille 1981] (Lille, 1984).

3. Aarsleff *et al.* (1987)★

4. Dutz, Klaus D., ed., *Speculum historiographiae linguisticae: Kurzbeiträge der IV. Internationalen Konferenz zur Geschichte der Sprachwissenschaften (ICHoLS IV) Trier, 24.–27. August 1987* (Münster, 1989).

5. Niederehe, Hans-Josef and E. F. Konrad Koerner, eds, *History and Historiography of Linguistics* [ICHoLS IV, Trier 1987], SHLS, 51 (Amsterdam, 1990).

6. Ahlqvist, Anders *et al.,* eds, *Diversions of Galway: Papers on the History of Linguistics. From ICHoLS V, Galway, Ireland, 1–6 September 1990,* SHLS, 68 (Amsterdam, 1992).

7. Bynon-Palmer*
8. Hüllen, Werner, ed., *Understanding the Historiography of Linguistics. Problems and Projects. Symposium at Essen, 23–25 November 1989* (Münster, 1990).
9. Hymes, Dell, ed., *Studies in the History of Linguistics: Traditions and Paradigms* (Bloomington, Ind., 1975).
10. Parret*
11. Ricken, Ulrich, ed., "Philosophische Positionen und Kontroversen in der Sprachwissenschaft" [Colloquium at Halle, 11–12 Dec. 1975], *Zeitschrift für Phonetik, Sprachwissenschaft und Kommunikationsforschung*, 29, nos 5/6 (1976).
12. Rosier, Irène, ed., *L'Héritage des grammairiens latins de l'antiquité aux lumières. Actes du Colloque de Chantilly 2–4 septembre 1987* (Paris, 1988).

5. History of English language scholarship

1. Kennedy*, 12413–57.
2. McArthur, Tom, ed., *The Oxford Companion to the English Language* (Oxford, 1992).
3. Bailey, Richard W., *Images of English: A Cultural History of the Language* (Ann Arbor, Michigan, 1991).
4. Baugh-Cable*
5. Bolton and Crystal (1966–1969) [cf. 30.6. and 70.6.]
6. Flügel, Ewald, "The History of English Philology," in *Flügel Memorial Volume,* Leland Stanford Junior University Publications (Stanford, Calif., 1916), pp. 9–35.
7. Howatt*
8. Kühlwein, Wolfgang, *Linguistics in Great Britain,* 2 vols (Tübingen, 1970–1971).
9. Welte, Werner, *Die englische Gebrauchsgrammatik,* Teil I: Geschichte und Grundannahmen, Studien zur englischen Grammatik, 1,1 (Tübingen, 1985).
10. Michael, Ian, ed., *Early textbooks of English: a guide* (Reading, 1993).
11. Murphy, James J., ed., *A Short History of Writing Instruction* (Davis, Calif., 1990).

6. Biographies of linguists
— see also section 71 —

1. Kennedy*, 12835–983.
2. Sebeok, Thomas Albert, *Portraits of Linguists: A Biographical Source Book for the History of Western Linguistics, 1746–1963,* 2 vols (Bloomington, Ind., 1966).
3. *Dictionary of National Biography,* ed. Leslie Stephen and Sidney Lee, 63 vols (London, 1885–1900), with *Supplement,* 3 vols (1901) repr. in 22 vols (1908–1909); *Errata* (1904); continued in further supplements until 1985.
4. *Dictionary of American Biography,* ed. Allen Johnson and Dumas Malone, 20 vols (New York and London, 1928–1936); *Index* (Oxford, 1937), eight *Supplements* (1944–1988) [covering the period up to 1970].
5. Haenicke, Gunta and Thomas Finkenstaedt, *Anglistenlexikon 1825– 1990. Biographische und bibliographische Angaben zu 318 Anglisten,* Augsburger I&I-Schriften, 64 (Augsburg, 1992). [Includes Austrian, German and Swiss scholars]
6. McArthur (1992) [cf. 5.2.]

7. The study of language in the Middle Ages

1. Koerner, Konrad, "Medieval Linguistic Thought: A Comprehensive Bibliography," in Koerner *et al.* (1980) [cf. 17.9.], pp. 265–99.
2. Bursill-Hall, Geoffrey L., *A Census of Medieval Latin Grammatical Manuscripts,* Grammatica speculativa, 4 (Stuttgart/Bad Cannstadt, 1981). [Review by F. J. Worstbrock, *Arbitrium,* 1 (1983), 15–24.]
3. Arens (1969)*, part one, ch. II.
4. Robins (1990)*, ch. 4.
5. Abelson, Paul, *The Seven Liberal Arts: A Study in Medieval Culture* (New York, 1906).
6. Baebler, Johann J., *Beiträge zu einer Geschichte der lateinischen Grammatik im Mittelalter* (Halle, 1885).
7. Bursill-Hall, Geoffrey L., "The Middle Ages," in Sebeok (1975)*, pp. 179–230.
8. Curtius, Ernst Robert, *European Literature and the Latin Middle Ages,* trans. Willard R. Trask (New York, 1953).
9. Illmer, Detlef, *Formen der Erziehung und Wissensvermittlung im frühen Mittelalter: Quellenstudien zur Frage der Kontinuität des abendländischen*

Erziehungswesens, Münchener Beiträge zur Mediävistik und Renaissance-Forschung, 7 (Munich, 1971).

10. Irvine, Martin, *The Making of Textual Culture. 'Grammatica' and Literary Theory, 350–1100,* Cambridge Studies in Medieval Literature, 19 (Cambridge, 1994).

11. Kukenheim (1951) [cf. 28.10.]

12. Manitius*

13. Paetow, Louis John, *The Arts Course at Medieval Universities with Special Reference to Grammar and Rhetoric,* University Studies of the University of Illinois, vol. 3, no. 7 (Urbana, Ill., 1910).

14. Robins, Robert H., *Ancient and Mediaeval Grammatical Theory in Europe: With Particular Reference to Modern Linguistic Doctrine* (London, 1951).

15. Thurot, Charles, *Extraits de divers manuscrits latins pour servir à l'histoire des doctrines grammaticales du moyen âge,* Notices et extraits, 22 (Paris, 1869).

16. Ebbesen, Sten, ed., *Sprachtheorien in Spätantike und Mittelalter,* Geschichte der Sprachtheorie, 3 (Tübingen, 1995).

17. Law, Vivien, ed., *History of Linguistic Thought in the Early Middle Ages,* SHLS, 71 (Amsterdam, 1993). This includes "The Historiography of Grammar in the Early Middle Ages" (pp. 1–23), and "Grammar in the Early Middle Ages: A Bibliography" (pp. 25–47), both by V. Law.

18. Lepschy (1994) [cf. 4.11.]

8. The Roman grammarians

1. *RE**

2. Arens (1969)*, pp. 3–34.

3. Robins (1990)*, chs. 2 and 3.

4. Gudeman, Alfred, "Grammatik," in *RE**, VII/ii (1912) [= 14. Halbband], 1780–1811.

5. Jeep, Ludwig, *Zur Geschichte der Lehre von den Redetheilen bei den lateinischen Grammatikern* (Leipzig, 1893).

6. Law (1982) [cf. 9.3.], ch. II.

7. Law, Vivien, "Late Latin Grammars in the Early Middle Ages: A Typological History," in *The History of Linguistics in the Classical Period,* ed. Daniel J. Taylor, SHLS, 46 (Amsterdam, 1987), pp. 191–206.

8. Manitius*, vol. I (1911).

9. Robins (1951) [cf. 7.14.]

10. Romeo, Luigi, "Classical Antiquity: Rome," in Sebeok (1975)★, pp. 127–77.

11. Romeo, Luigi and Gaio E. Tiberio, "Historiography of Linguistics and Rome's Scholarship," *Language Sciences,* 17 (1971), 23–44.

12. Sandys, John Edwin, *A History of Classical Scholarship,* 3 vols (Cambridge, I: third ed. 1921; II and III: 1908), vol. I, book III.

13. Scaglione, Aldo D., *Ars Grammatica: A Bibliographic Survey, Two Essays on the Grammar of the Latin and Italian Subjunctive, and a Note on the Ablative Absolute,* JL, Series Minor, 77 (The Hague, 1970), ch. I.

14. Schanz, Martin, *Geschichte der römischen Literatur bis zum Gesetzgebungswerk des Kaisers Justinian,* rev. Karl Hosius and Gustav Krüger, 3 vols, Handbuch der Altertumswissenschaft, 8/III, IV (Munich, III: third ed. 1922; IV.i: sec. ed. 1914; IV.ii: 1920).

15. Schmidt, Peter Lebrecht, "Grammatik und Rhetorik," in *Restauration und Erneuerung: Die lateinische Literatur von 284 bis 374 n. Chr.,* ed. Reinhart Herzog, Handbuch der lateinischen Literatur der Antike, vol. 5 (Munich, 1989), pp. 101–60.

16. Amsler, Mark, *Etymology and Grammatical Discourse in Late Antiquity and the Middle Ages,* SHLS, 44 (Amsterdam, 1989).

17. Kaster, Robert A., *Guardians of Language: The Grammarian and Society in Late Antiquity* (Berkeley, Calif., 1988).

18. *Grammatici latini,* ed. Heinrich Keil, Martin Hertz and Hermann Hagen, 8 vols (Leipzig, 1855–1880; repr. Hildesheim, 1961).

19. Holtz, Louis, *Donat et la tradition de l'enseignement grammatical* (Paris, 1981).

20. *The* Ars minor *of Donatus,* trans. and introd. Wayland J. Chase, University of Wisconsin Studies in the Social Sciences and History, 11 (Madison, Wisconsin, 1926).

21. Lomanto, Valeria and Nino Marinone, eds, *Index Grammaticus: An Index to Latin Grammar Texts,* 3 vols (Hildesheim, 1990).

22. Schmitter, Peter, ed., *Sprachtheorien der abendländischen Antike,* Geschichte der Sprachtheorie, 2 (Tübingen, 1991).

9. The study of language in early Anglo-Saxon England

1. Reinsma, Luke, "Rhetoric, Grammar and Literature in England and Ireland before the Norman Conquest: A Select Bibliography," *Rhetoric Society Quarterly,* 8, no. 1 (1978), 29–48.

2. Gneuss (1990)★

3. Law, Vivien, *The Insular Latin Grammarians* (Woodbridge, Suffolk, 1982).
4. Law, Vivien, "The Study of Latin Grammar in Eighth-Century Southumbria," *ASE,* 12 (1983), 43–71.
5. Riché, Pierre, *Education and Culture in the Barbarian West from the Sixth through Eighth Centuries,* trans. from the third ed. John J. Contreni (Columbia, S. C., 1976).
6. Roger, Maurice, *L'enseignement des lettres classiques d'Ausone à Alcuin: Introduction à l'histoire des écoles carolingiennes* (Paris, 1905), ch. VII.
7. *Bonifatii (Vynfreth) Ars Grammatica,* ed. George John Gebauer and Bengt Löfstedt, CC Series Latina, 133B (Turnhout, 1980).
8. *Tatvini Opera omnia; Variae collectiones aenigmatum Merovingicae aetatis; Anonymus de dubiis nominibus,* ed. Maria de Marco and Fr. Glorie, 2 vols, CC Series Latina, 133 and 133A (Turnhout, 1968); *Ars Tatvini,* ed. M. de Marco, I, 1–93.
9. *Aldhelm: The Prose Works,* trans. [and introd.] Michael Lapidge and Michael Herren (Cambridge, 1979).
10. *Aldhelm: The Poetic Works,* trans. Michael Lapidge and James L. Rosier [introd. Michael Lapidge] (Cambridge, 1985).
11. Brown, George Hardin, *Bede the Venerable* (Boston, 1987), ch. 2.
12. Irvine, Martin, "Bede the Grammarian and the Scope of Grammatical Studies in Eighth-Century Northumbria," *ASE,* 15 (1986), 15–44.

10. Irish Latin grammarians

1. Lapidge, Michael and Richard Sharpe, *A Bibliography of Celtic-Latin Literature 400–1200,* Royal Irish Academy Dictionary of Medieval Latin from Celtic Sources, Ancillary Publications, 1 (Dublin, 1985). [Review by Michael Herren, *Peritia,* 5 (1986), 422–7.]
2. Law (1982) [cf. 9.3.]
3. Manitius*, vol. I (1911).
4. Holtz, Louis, "Les grammairiens Hiberno-Latins: Etaient-ils des Anglo-Saxons?," *Peritia,* 2 (1983), 170–84.
5. Schmidt (1989) [cf. 8.15.], pp. 146–7.
6. *Anonymus ad Cuimnanum: Expossitio Latinitatis,* ed. Bernhard Bischoff and Bengt Löfstedt, CC Series Latina, 133D (Turnhout, 1992).
7. *Grammatici Hibernici Carolini aevi,* ed. Louis Holtz, B. Löfstedt and John Chittenden, 5 vols, CC Continuatio Mediaevalis, 40–40D (Turnhout, 1977–1982).

8. Löfstedt, Bengt, *Der hibernolateinische Grammatiker Malsachanus,* Acta Universitatis Upsaliensis, Studia Latina Upsaliensia, 3 (Uppsala, 1965).

11. Later Anglo-Saxon England; Abbo of Fleury, Ælfric
— see also Reinsma and Gneuss in section 9 —

1. *Abbon de Fleury: Questions grammaticales,* ed. Anita Guerreau-Jalabert (Paris, 1982).
2. Funke, Otto, *Die gelehrten lateinischen Lehn- und Fremdwörter in der altenglischen Literatur* . . . *nebst einer einleitenden Abhandlung über die "Quaestiones grammaticales" des Abbo Floriacensis* (Halle, 1914).
3. Mostert, Marco, "Le séjour d'Abbon de Fleury à Ramsey," *Bibliothéque de l'École des Chartes,* 144 (1986), 199–208.
4. *Ælfrics Grammatik und Glossar, Erste Abteilung: Text und Varianten,* ed. Julius Zupitza (Berlin, 1880); repr. with introductory material by Helmut Gneuss (Berlin, 1966).
5. Reinsma, Luke M., *Ælfric: An Annotated Bibliography* (New York, 1987), pp. 183–90.
6. Bullough, Donald A., "The Educational Tradition in England from Alfred to Aelfric: Teaching *utriusque linguae,*" in *Settimane di studio del Centro italiano di studi sull'alto medioevo,* XIX, 1971 (Spoleto, 1972), 453–94, esp. pp. 488–9.
7. T. Hunt★, vol. I, ch. 5.
8. Law, Vivien, "Anglo-Saxon England: Aelfric's 'Excerptiones de arte grammatica anglice'," *Histoire, Épistémologie, Langage,* 9 (1987), 47–71.
9. Pàroli, Teresa, "Le opere grammaticali di Ælfric," *Annali Istituto Universitario Orientale di Napoli: Sezione Germanica,* 10 (1967), 5–43, and 11 (1968), 35–133.
10. Williams, Edna Rees, "Ælfric's Grammatical Terminology," *PMLA,* 73 (1958), 453–62.
11. Gneuss, Helmut, "The Origin of Standard Old English and Æthelwold's School at Winchester," *ASE,* 1 (1972), 63–83.
12. Hofstetter, Walter, *Winchester und der spätaltenglische Sprachgebrauch: Untersuchungen zur geographischen und zeitlichen Verbreitung altenglischer Synonyme,* TUEPh, 14 (Munich, 1987).
13. Hofstetter, Walter, "Winchester and the Standardization of Old English Vocabulary," *ASE,* 17 (1988), 139–61.
14. Bayless, Martha, "*Beatus quid est* and the Study of Grammar in Late Anglo-Saxon England," in Law (1993) [cf. 7.17.], pp. 67–110.

12. Synonymy and *Differentia* in the Middle Ages

1. Gneuss (1990)★, pp. 25–7.
2. Goetz, Georg, "Differentiarum scriptores," in *RE*★, V/i (1903) [= 9. Halbband], 481–4.
3. Brugnoli, Giorgio, *Studi sulle "Differentiae Verborum"* (Rome, 1955).
4. Law, Vivien and James P. Carley, "Grammar and Arithmetic in Two Thirteenth-Century English Monastic Collections," *The Journal of Medieval Latin*, 1 (1991), 140–67, at 150–1.
5. *De proprietate sermonum vel rerum: A Study and Critical Edition of a Set of Verbal Distinctions,* ed. Myra L. Uhlfelder, Papers and Monographs of the American Academy in Rome, 15 (Rome, 1954), "Introduction".
6. Hofstetter (1987) [cf. 11.12.]
   See also the literature on John of Garland and the Latin dictionaries of the later Middle Ages (sections 19 and 25).

13. Medieval rhetoric

1. Murphy, James J., *Medieval Rhetoric: A Select Bibliography,* sec. ed. (Toronto, 1989).
2. Baldwin, Charles Sears, *Medieval Rhetoric and Poetic (to 1400) Interpreted from Representative Works* (New York, 1928).
3. Curtius (1953) [cf. 7.8.], ch. 4.
4. Kennedy, George A., *Classical Rhetoric and its Christian and Secular Tradition from Ancient to Modern Times* (Chapel Hill, N. C., 1980).
5. *Readings in Medieval Rhetoric,* ed. Joseph M. Miller, Michael H. Prosser and Thomas W. Benson (Bloomington, Ind., 1973).
6. Murphy, James J., ed., *Medieval Eloquence: Studies in the Theory and Practice of Medieval Rhetoric* (Berkeley, Calif., 1978).
7. Murphy, James J., *Rhetoric in the Middle Ages: A History of Rhetorical Theory from Saint Augustine to the Renaissance* (Berkeley, Calif., 1974), esp. chs III–VI.
8. Murphy, James J., "The Middle Ages," in Horner (1983) [cf. 39.6.], pp. 40–74.
9. Payne, Robert O., "Chaucer and the Art of Rhetoric," in *Companion to Chaucer Studies,* ed. Beryl Rowland, rev. ed. (New York, 1979), pp. 42–64.
10. Vickers, Brian, *In Defence of Rhetoric* (Oxford, 1988).

11. Knappe, Gabriele, *Traditionen der klassischen Rhetorik im angelsächsischen England* (Heidelberg, 1995).
12. Gneuss (1990)⋆, pp. 28–32.
13. Kennedy, George A., *The Art of Rhetoric in the Roman World: 300 BC–AD 300*, A History of Rhetoric, 2 (Princeton, N. J., 1972).
14. Ueding, Gert, ed., *Historisches Wörterbuch der Rhetorik*, 8 vols (Tübingen, 1992–). [Vol. I published]

14. Latin and Anglo-Saxon glossography

1. Kennedy⋆, 3783–902.
2. Goetz, Georg, "Glossographie," in *RE*⋆, VII/i (1910) [= 13. Halbband], 1433–66.
3. Goetz, Georg, *Corpus glossariorum latinorum*, vol. I: *De glossariorum latinorum origine et fatis* (Leipzig, 1923).
4. Tolkiehn, J., "Lexikographie," in *RE*⋆, XII/ii (1925) [= 24. Halbband], 2432–82.
5. Buridant, Claude, "Lexicographie et glossographie médiévales: Esquisse de bilan et perspectives de recherche," in *La lexicographie au moyen âge,* ed. Claude Buridant, Lexique, 4 (Lille, 1986), pp. 9–46.
6. Cameron, Angus, "A List of Old English Texts," in *A Plan for the Dictionary of Old English,* ed. Roberta Frank and Angus Cameron (Toronto, 1973), pp. 248–54. [Latin–Old English glossaries]
7. Campbell, A., *Old English Grammar* (Oxford, 1959), pp. 359–60.
8. Pheifer, J. D., ed., *Old English Glosses in the Épinal-Erfurt Glossary* (Oxford, 1974).
9. Lapidge, Michael, "The School of Theodore and Hadrian," *ASE,* 15 (1986), 45–72.
10. Pheifer, J. D., "Early Anglo-Saxon Glossaries and the School of Canterbury," *ASE,* 16 (1987), 17–44.
11. Gneuss (1990)⋆, pp. 18–22.

15. Glossing, translation and the knowledge of foreign languages, especially in early medieval England

1. Gneuss, Helmut, "Bücher und Leser in England im 10. Jahrhundert," in *Medialität und mittelalterliche insulare Literatur,* ed. Hildegard L. C. Tristram, ScriptOralia, 43 (Tübingen, 1992), pp. 104–30.

2. Lapidge, Michael, "The Study of Latin Texts in Late Anglo-Saxon England [1]: The Evidence of Latin Glosses," and R. I. Page, "The Study ... [2]: The Evidence of English Glosses," in *Latin and the Vernacular Languages in Early Medieval Britain,* ed. Nicholas Brooks (Leicester, 1982), pp. 99–140 and 141–65.

3. Wieland, Gernot Rudolf, *The Latin Glosses on Arator and Prudentius in Cambridge University Library, MS Gg.5.35,* Studies and Texts, 61 (Toronto, 1983).

4. Korhammer, Michael, *Die monastischen Cantica im Mittelalter und ihre altenglischen Interlinearversionen: Studien und Textausgabe,* TUEPh, 6 (Munich, 1976), pp. 129–37.

5. Korhammer, Michael, "Mittelalterliche Konstruktionshilfen und altenglische Wortstellung," *Scriptorium,* 34 (1980), 18–58.

6. Amos, Flora Ross, *Early Theories of Translation* (New York, 1920).

7. Ellis, Roger, ed., *The Medieval Translator: The Theory and Practice of Translation in the Middle Ages. Papers Read at a Conference Held 20–23 August 1987 at the University of Wales Conference Centre, Gregynog Hall* (Cambridge, 1989).

8. Marsden, Richard, "Ælfric as Translator: The Old English Prose Genesis," *Anglia,* 109 (1991), 319–58.

9. Minkoff, Harvey, "Some Stylistic Consequences of Ælfric's Theory of Translation," *SP,* 73 (1976), 29–41.

10. Sauer, Hans, ed., *Theodulfi Capitula in England: Die altenglischen Übersetzungen, zusammen mit dem lateinischen Text,* TUEPh, 8 (Munich, 1978), pp. 118–74.

11. Sauer, Hans, "Die 72 Völker und Sprachen der Welt: Ein mittelalterlicher Topos in der englischen Literatur," *Anglia,* 101 (1983), 29–48, and "Die 72 Völker und Sprachen der Welt: Einige Ergänzungen," *Anglia,* 107 (1989), 61–4.

12. Gneuss, Helmut, "*Anglicae linguae interpretatio:* Language Contact, Lexical Borrowing and Glossing in Anglo-Saxon England," *Proceedings of the British Academy,* 82 (1993), 107–48.

13. Bischoff, Bernhard, "The Study of Foreign Languages in the Middle

Ages," *Speculum,* 36 (1961), 209–24. [Expanded version in B. Bischoff, *Mittelalterliche Studien: Ausgewählte Aufsätze zur Schriftkunde und Literaturgeschichte,* 3 vols (Stuttgart, 1966–1981), II (1967), 227–45.]

14. Bodden, Mary Catherine, "Evidence for Knowledge of Greek in Anglo-Saxon England," *ASE,* 17 (1988), 217–46.

15. Thiel, Matthias, *Grundlagen und Gestalt der Hebräischkenntnisse des frühen Mittelalters* (Spoleto, 1970).

16. Etymology in the Middle Ages

1. Brinkmann★, pp. 39–43.

2. Engels, Joseph, "La portée de l'étymologie Isidorienne," *Studi Medievali,* 3ª ser., 3 (1962), 99–128.

3. Gneuss (1990)★, pp. 22–5.

4. Klinck, Roswitha, *Die lateinische Etymologie des Mittelalters* (Munich, 1970).

5. Opelt, I., "Etymologie," in *Reallexikon für Antike und Christentum,* VI (1966), 797–844.

6. De Poerck, Guy, "Etymologia et origo à travers la tradition Latine," in *ANAMNHCIC: Gedenkboek Prof. Dr. E. A. Leemans,* Rijksuniversiteit te Gent. Werken uitgegeven door de Faculteit van de Letteren en Wijsbegeerte, 149 (Bruges, 1970), pp. 191–228.

7. Sanders, Willy, "Grundzüge und Wandlungen der Etymologie," in *Etymologie,* ed. Rüdiger Schmitt, Wege der Forschung, 373 (Darmstadt, 1977), pp. 7–49.

8. Wölfflin, Eduard, "Die Etymologien der lateinischen Grammatiker," *Archiv für lateinische Lexikographie und Grammatik,* 8 (1893), 421–40 and 563–85.

17. The later Middle Ages in England
— see also section 7 —

1. Baugh-Cable★, chs 5–7.

2. Bursill-Hall (1981) [cf. 7.2.]

3. Cavanaugh, Susan Hagen, "A Study of Books Privately Owned in England: 1300–1450" (Ph.D. Dissertation, University of Pennsylvania, 1980).

4. Brinkmann★, pp. 21–51.

5. Coleman, Janet, *English Literature in History 1350–1400: Medieval Readers and Writers* (London, 1981), ch. 2: "Vernacular Literacy and Lay Education".

6. Hunt, Richard W., *Collected Papers on the History of Grammar in the Middle Ages*, SHLS, 5 (Amsterdam, 1980); "Additions and Corrections," ed. M. T. Gibson and S. P. Hall, *Bodleian Library Record*, 11 (1982–1985), 9–19.

7. Kukenheim (1951) [cf. 28.10.]

8. Manitius★, vol. III (1931), 175–220 and 719–62.

9. Koerner, Konrad, H. J. Niederehe and R. H. Robins, eds, *Studies in Medieval Linguistic Thought Dedicated to Geoffrey L. Bursill-Hall*, SHLS, 26 (Amsterdam, 1980) [= *HL*, 7, nos 1/2 (1980)].

10. Wilson, R. M., "The Contents of the Medieval Library," in *The English Library before 1700: Studies in its History*, ed. Francis Wormald and C. E. Wright (London, 1958), pp. 86–111, at 101–2.

11. Bennett, H. S., *English Books and Readers 1475 to 1557: Being a Study in the History of the Book Trade from Caxton to the Incorporation of the Stationer's Company*, sec. ed. (Cambridge, 1969), esp. chs II and VI.3.

12. T. Hunt★

13. Leach, A. F., *The Schools of Medieval England*, sec. ed. (London, 1916).

14. Miner, John M., *The Grammar Schools of Medieval England: A. F. Leach in Historical Perspective* (Montreal, 1990), chs 6 and 7.

15. Orme, Nicholas, *English Schools in the Middle Ages* (London, 1973).

16. Orme, Nicholas, *Education and Society in Medieval and Renaissance England* (London, 1989).

17. Moran, Jo Ann H., *The Growth of English Schooling 1340–1548: Learning, Literacy and Laicization in Pre-Reformation York Diocese* (Princeton, N. J., 1985), ch. 2.

18. Tolkien, J. R. R., "Chaucer as a Philologist: *The Reeve's Tale*," TPS (1934), 1–70.

— Orm —

19. *Early Middle English Verse and Prose*, ed. J. A. W. Bennett and G. V. Smithers, sec. ed. (Oxford, 1968), pp. 360–1.

— The 'Tremulous Hand' —

20. Crawford, S. J., "The Worcester Marks and Glosses of the Old English Manuscripts in the Bodleian," *Anglia*, 52 (1928), 1–25.

21. Gneuss, Helmut, "Englands Bibliotheken im Mittelalter und ihr Untergang," in *Festschrift für Walter Hübner*, ed. Dieter Riesner and Helmut Gneuss (Berlin, 1964), pp. 91–121, at 100–101.

22. Franzen, Christine, *The Tremulous Hand of Worcester. A Study of Old English in the Thirteenth Century* (Oxford, 1991).

18. The study of French in medieval England

1. Baugh-Cable★, chs 5–7.
2. Brunner, Karl, *Die englische Sprache: Ihre geschichtliche Entwicklung,* sec. ed., 2 vols (Tübingen, 1960–1962), I (1960), 120–1.
3. T. Hunt★
4. Käsmann, Hans, *Studien zum kirchlichen Wortschatz des Mittelenglischen 1100–1350: Ein Beitrag zum Problem der Sprachmischung* (Tübingen, 1961).
5. Kibbee, Douglas A., *For to Speke Frenche Trewely. The French Language in England, 1000–1600: Its Status, Description and Instruction,* SHLS, 60 (Amsterdam, 1991).
6. Koch, Johann, "Der anglonormannische Traktat des Walter von Bibbesworth in seiner Bedeutung für die Anglistik," *Anglia,* 58 (1934), 30–77.
7. Lambley, K., *The Teaching and Cultivation of the French Language in England during Tudor and Stuart Times,* Publications of the University of Manchester, 129 (Manchester, 1920).
8. Rothwell, William, "The Teaching of French in Medieval England," *Modern Language Review,* 63 (1968), 37–46.
9. Streuber, Albert, "Die ältesten Anleitungsschriften zur Erlernung des Französischen in England und den Niederlanden bis zum 16. Jahrhundert," *Zeitschrift für französische Sprache und Literatur,* 72 (1962), 37–86.
10. Berkhout, Carl T., "Stephen Batman and the *Expositio Vocabulorum,*" *Neophilologus,* 69 (1985), 476–8.
11. *Dialogues in French and English by William Caxton,* ed. Henry Bradley, Early English Text Society, E. S. 79 (London, 1900). [See also *Le livre des mestiers de Bruges et ses dérivés: Quatre anciens manuels de conversation,* ed. Jean Gessler (Bruges, 1931), C: Caxton's *Dialogues* and Introduction, pp. 31–42.]
12. Skeat, W. W., ed., "Nominale sive Verbale," *TPS* (1903–1906), ★1–★50.

19. Grammars and textbooks of Latin in the Middle English period

1. Bursill-Hall, Geoffrey L., "Teaching Grammars of the Middle Ages: Notes on the Manuscript Tradition," *HL,* 4 (1977), 1–29.

— Petrus Helias —

2. "Petrus Helias' 'Summa Super Priscianum' I–III: An Edition and Study," ed. Leo Alexander Reilly (Ph. D. Dissertation, University of Toronto, 1975).

3. *The* Summa *of Petrus Helias on Priscian Minor,* ed. James E. Tolson, with an introd. to part II by M. Gibson, Cahiers de l'Institut du Moyen Âge Grec et Latin, 27/28 (Copenhagen, 1978).

4. Hunt, Richard W., "Hugutio and Petrus Helias," in Hunt, *Collected Papers* (1980) [cf. 17.6.], pp. 145–9. See also Manitius★, vol. III (1931), 184–7, and Dinneen (1967) [cf. 4.7.], pp. 128–32.

— Alexander de Villa Dei —

5. *Das* Doctrinale *des Alexander de Villa-Dei: Kritisch-exegetische Ausgabe,* ed. D. Reichling, Monumenta Germaniae Paedagogica, 12 (Berlin, 1893). See also Manitius★, vol. III (1931), 756–61.

— Evrard de Béthune —

6. *Eberhardi Bethuniensis Graecismus,* ed. J. Wrobel, Corpus grammaticorum medii aevi, 1 (Breslau, 1887). See also Manitius★, vol. III (1931), 747–51, and U. Kindermann, in *Lexikon des Mittelalters,* III (1986), 1523.

— John of Garland, Alexander Neckam and Adam de Parvo Ponte —

7. T. Hunt★

8. Worstbrock, F. J., "Johannes de Garlandia," in *Die deutsche Literatur des Mittelalters: Verfasserlexikon,* sec. ed., IV (1983), 612–23.

9. Born, Lester K., "The Manuscripts of the Major Grammatical Works of John of Garland," *Transactions and Proceedings of the American Philological Association,* 69 (1938), 259–73.

10. Brinkmann★, pp. 43–4 and n.

11. Bursill-Hall, G. L., "Johannes de Garlandia—Forgotten Grammarian and the Manuscript Tradition," *HL,* 3 (1976), 155–77, and "Johannes de Garlandia: Additional Manuscript Material," *HL,* 6 (1979), 77–86.

12. Habel, Edwin, "Johannes de Garlandia, ein Schulmann des 13. Jahrhunderts," *Mitteilungen der Gesellschaft für deutsche Erziehungs- und Schulgeschichte,* 19 (1909), 1–34 and 118–30.

13. *Morale Scolarium of John of Garland (Johannes de Garlandia): A Professor in the Universities of Paris and Toulouse in the Thirteenth Century,* ed. and introd. Louis John Paetow, Memoirs of the University of California, 4,2 (Berkeley, Calif., 1927), part I.

14. *The Dictionarius of John de Garlande and the Author's Commentary,* trans. and annot. Barbara Blatt Rubin (Lawrence, Kansas, 1981).

15. Hunt, R. W., *The Schools and the Cloister: The Life and Writings of Alexander Nequam (1157–1217),* ed. and rev. Margaret Gibson (Oxford, 1984 [originally a D. Phil. Dissertation, Oxford, 1936]). See also Manitius★, vol. III (1931), 784–94.

16. Scheler, August, "Trois traités de lexicographie latine du XIIᵉ et du XIIIᵉ siècle," *Jahrbuch für romanische und englische Literatur,* 6 (1865), 43–59, 142–62, 287–321, 370–9; 7 (1866), 58–74, 155–73, and 8 (1867), 75–93. [Editions of John of Garland, *Dictionarius,* Alexander Neckam and Adam de Parvo Ponte]

17. *A Volume of Vocabularies . . . ,* ed. Thomas Wright, 2 vols (1857–1873), I (1857). [Includes editions of John of Garland, *Dictionarius, Distigium sive Cornutus,* and Alexander Neckam, *De nominibus utensilium*]

18. Manitius★, vol. III (1931), 202–4. [On Adam de Parvo Ponte]

20. Speculative Grammar

1. Ashworth, Earline J., *The Tradition of Medieval Logic and Speculative Grammar from Anselm to the End of the Seventeenth Century: A Bibliography from 1836 onwards,* Subsidia Mediaevalia, 9 (Toronto, 1978).

2. Bursill-Hall, G. L., *Speculative Grammars of the Middle Ages: The Doctrine of partes orationis of the Modistae,* Approaches to Semiotics, 11 (The Hague, 1971).

3. Covington, Michael A., *Syntactic Theory in the High Middle Ages: Modistic Models of Sentence Structure,* Cambridge Studies in Linguistics, 39 (Cambridge, 1984).

4. Covington, Michael A., "Grammatical Theory in the Middle Ages," in Bynon-Palmer★, pp. 23–42.

5. Enders, Heinz W., *Sprachlogische Traktate des Mittelalters und der Semantikbegriff: Ein historisch-systematischer Beitrag zur Frage der semantischen Grundlegung formaler Systeme,* Münchener Universitäts-Schriften, Fachbereich Katholische Theologie, Veröffentlichungen des Grabmann-Institutes zur Erforschung der mittelalterlichen Theologie und Philosophie, N. F., 20 (Paderborn, 1975).

6. Grabmann, Martin, "Die Entwicklung der mittelalterlichen Sprachlogik," in *Mittelalterliches Geistesleben: Abhandlungen zur Geschichte der Scholastik und Mystik* (Munich, 1926), ch. IV.

7. Pérez Rodríguez, E., "Modisten," in *Lexikon des Mittelalters,* VI (1992), 710–11.
8. Pinborg, Jan, *Die Entwicklung der Sprachtheorie im Mittelalter,* Beiträge zur Geschichte der Philosophie und Theologie des Mittelalters, Texte und Untersuchungen, 42,2 (Copenhagen, 1967).
9. Pinborg, Jan, *Logik und Semantik im Mittelalter: Ein Überblick* (Stuttgart/Bad Cannstatt, 1972).
10. Robins (1990)*, ch. 4.
11. Rosier, Irène E., *La grammaire spéculative des Modistes* (Lille, 1983).
12. Thomas of Erfurt, *Grammatica speculativa,* ed. with translation and commentary G. L. Bursill-Hall (London, 1972).
13. Bursill-Hall, G. L., Sten Ebbesen and Konrad Koerner, eds, *De ortu grammaticae: Studies in Medieval Grammar and Linguistic Theory in Memory of Jan Pinborg,* SHLS, 43 (Amsterdam, 1990).

21. Latin grammars in English
(from the 14th century onwards)

1. Orme (1973) [cf. 17.15.]
2. Lewis, R. E., N. F. Blake and A. S. G. Edwards, *Index of Printed Middle English Prose* (New York, 1985).
3. Thomson, David, *A Descriptive Catalogue of Middle English Grammatical Texts* (New York, 1979).
4. *An Edition of the Middle English Grammatical Texts,* ed. David Thomson, Garland Medieval Texts, 8 (New York, 1984).
5. Bland, Cynthia Renée, *The Teaching of Grammar in Late Medieval England. An Edition, with Commentary, of Oxford, Lincoln College MS Lat. 130* (East Lansing, Michigan, 1991).
6. Bland, Cynthia Renée, "John of Cornwall's Innovations and their Possible Effects on Chaucer," in *The Uses of Manuscripts in Literary Studies. Essays in Memory of Judson Boyce Allen,* ed. Charlotte Cook Morse, Penelope Reed Doob and Marjorie Curry Woods (Kalamazoo, Michigan, 1992), pp. 213–35.
7. Brother Bonaventure [= John M. Miner], "The Teaching of Latin in Later Medieval England," *Mediaeval Studies,* 23 (1961), 1–20.
8. Gwosdek, Hedwig, ed., *Early Printed Editions of the Long Accidence Grammars,* Anglistische Forschungen, 213 (Heidelberg, 1991).
9. Meech, Sanford B., "Early Application of Latin Grammar to English," *PMLA,* 50 (1935), 1012–32.

10. Meech, Sanford B., "John Drury and his English Writings," *Speculum*, 9 (1934), 70–83.
11. Meech, Sanford B., "An Early Treatise in English Concerning Latin Grammar," in *Essays and Studies in English and Comparative Literature*, University of Michigan Publications, Language and Literature, 13 (Ann Arbor, Michigan, 1935), pp. 81–125.
12. Smyly, J. Gilbart, "A Latin Grammar in English," *Hermathena*, 20 (1930), 353–9.
13. Stevenson, W. H., "The Introduction of English as the Vehicle of Instruction in English Schools," in *An English Miscellany Presented to Dr. Furnivall in Honour of his Seventy-Fifth Birthday* (Oxford, 1901), pp. 421–9.
14. Thomson, David, "The Oxford Grammar Masters Revisited," *Mediaeval Studies*, 45 (1983), 298–310.

22. English grammatical terminology in late Middle English texts

1. Alford, John A., "The Grammatical Metaphor: A Survey of its Use in the Middle Ages," *Speculum*, 57 (1982), 728–60.
2. Amassian, Margaret and James Sadowsky, "Mede and Mercede: A Study of the Grammatical Metaphor in 'Piers Plowman' C: IV, 335–409," *NM*, 72 (1971), 457–76.
3. Kaske, R. E., " '*Ex Vi Transicionis*' and its Passage in *Piers Plowman*," *JEGP*, 62 (1963), 32–60.
4. Overstreet, Samuel A., "'Grammaticus Ludens': Theological Aspects of Langland's Grammatical Allegory," *Traditio*, 40 (1984), 251–96.

23. *Vulgaria*

1. Orme, Nicholas, "Latin and English Sentences in Fifteenth-Century Schoolbooks," and "A Transcript of the English and Latin Sentences in Beinecke Library MS 3 (34), Fol. 5," *The Yale University Library Gazette*, 60 (Oct. 1985), 47–57.
2. *Vulgaria viri doctissimi Guil. Hormani Caesarisburgensis (London, 1519)*, ed. and introd. Montague Rhodes James, Roxburghe Club, 139 (Oxford, 1926).
3. *A Fifteenth-Century School Book from a Manuscript in the British Museum (MS. Arundel 249)*, ed. William Nelson (Oxford, 1956).
4. Carlson, David R., "The 'Grammarians' War' 1519–1521, Humanist

Careerism in Early Tudor England, and Printing", *Medievalia et Humanistica*, N.S. 18 (1992), 157–81.

5. Orme, Nicholas, "An Early-Tudor Oxford Schoolbook," *Renaissance Quarterly*, 34 (1981), 11–39.
6. Orme, Nicholas, "A Grammatical Miscellany of 1427–1465 from Bristol and Wiltshire," *Traditio*, 38 (1982), 301–26.
7. *The Vulgaria of John Stanbridge and the Vulgaria of Robert Whittinton*, ed. Beatrice White, Early English Text Society, O. S. 187 (London, 1932), 1–30.
8. *The Winchester Anthology: A Facsimile of British Library Additional Manuscript 60577*, intro. Edward Wilson and Iain Fenlon (Cambridge, 1981). [Item 132: *Vulgaria*]

24. Glossaries and vocabularies in the Middle English period
— see also section 19 for John of Garland and Alexander Neckam —

1. Kennedy★, 5102–28.
2. Wright, Thomas, *Anglo-Saxon and Old English Vocabularies*, ed. and collated Richard Paul Wülcker, sec. ed., 2 vols (London, 1884).
3. Stein (1985)★, chs 8–10.
4. Miner (1990) [cf. 17.14.], pp. 163–6.
5. *English Glosses from British Library Additional Manuscript 37075*, ed. Thomas W. Ross and Edward Brooks, Jr (Norman, Oklahoma, 1984).
6. Voigts, Linda Ehrsam and Barbara A. Shailor, "The Recovery of a Fifteenth-Century Schoolmaster's Book: Beinecke MS 3, No. 34," *The Yale University Library Gazette*, 60 (Oct. 1985), 11–31.
7. Voigts, Linda Ehrsam, "A Letter from a Middle English Dictaminal Formulary in Harvard Law Library MS 43," *Speculum*, 56 (1981), 575–81.
8. Starnes-Noyes★, Appendix I.
9. Starnes (1954)★
10. Kuhn, Sherman M., "The Preface to a Fifteenth-Century Concordance," *Speculum*, 43 (1968), 258–73.

25. Latin dictionaries in the Middle Ages

1. Bursill-Hall (1981) [cf. 7.2.]
2. Goetz (1923) [cf. 14.3.]

3. Goetz (1910) [cf. 14.2.]
4. Manitius*, vol. II (1923), 717–24 [Papias]; vol. III (1931), 187–90 [Osbern], and 191–3 [Hugutio].
5. Brinkmann*, pp. 38–9, 78–82.
6. Buridant, Claude, ed., *La lexicographie au moyen âge,* Lexique, 4 (Lille, 1986).
7. Grubmüller, Klaus, "Überblick über die lateinische lexikographische Tradition bis zum Ende des 14. Jahrhunderts," in *Vocabularius ex quo: Untersuchungen zu lateinisch-deutschen Vokabularen des Spätmittelalters,* Münchener Texte und Untersuchungen zur deutschen Literatur des Mittelalters, 17 (Munich, 1967), pp. 13–30.
8. T. Hunt*, vol. I, ch. 17.
9. Weijers, Olga, *Dictionnaires et répertoires au moyen âge. Une étude du vocabulaire* (Turnhout, 1991).
10. Daly, Lloyd W. and B. A. Daly, "Some Techniques in Mediaeval Latin Lexicography," *Speculum,* 39, (1964), 229–39.
11. *Papiae Elementarium: Littera A,* ed. V. de Angelis, 3 vols, Testi e documenti per lo studio dell' Antichità, 58,1–3 (Milano, 1977–1980).
12. Riessner, Claus, *Die "Magnae derivationes" des Uguccione da Pisa und ihre Bedeutung für die romanische Philologie,* Temi e Testi, 11 (Rome, 1965).
13. *Summa Britonis sive Guillelmi Britonis Expositiones Vocabulorum Biblie,* ed. Lloyd W. Daly and Bernadine A. Daly, 2 vols, Thesaurus Mundi, 15 and 16 (Padua, 1975).
14. Grubmüller, Klaus, "Guilelmus Brito," in *Verfasserlexikon* [cf. 19.8.], III (1981), 300–2.

26. Medieval encyclopedias

1. Gruber, J., G. Bernt, J. Verger and K. Bitterling, "Enzyklopädie, Enzyklopädik," in *Lexikon des Mittelalters,* III (1986), 2031–9.
2. Beonio-Brocchieri Fumagalli, Maria Teresa, *Le enciclopedie dell' occidente medioevale,* Pedagogia, 20 (Turin, 1981).
3. Brinkmann*, pp. 76–8.
4. Collison, Robert, *Encyclopaedias: Their History throughout the Ages: A Bibliographical Guide with Extensive Historical Notes to the General Encyclopaedias Issued throughout the World from 350 B. C. to the Present Day,* sec. ed. (New York, 1966), ch. II.
5. Gandillac, Maurice de *et al., La pensée encyclopédique au moyen âge* (Neuchâtel, 1966).

6. Kren, Claudia, "Encyclopedic Tradition," in *Medieval Science and Technology: A Selected, Annotated Bibliography,* Bibliographies of the History of Science and Technology, 11, Garland Reference Library of the Humanities, 494 (New York, 1985), pp. 15–21.
7. Lawler, Traugott, "Encyclopedias and Dictionaries, Western Europe," in *Dictionary of the Middle Ages,* IV (1984), 447–50.
8. Meier, Christel, "Grundzüge der mittelalterlichen Enzyklopädik: Zu Inhalten, Formen und Funktionen einer problematischen Gattung," in *Literatur und Laienbildung im Spätmittelalter und in der Reformationszeit. Symposion Wolfenbüttel 1981,* ed. Ludger Grenzmann and Karl Stackmann (Stuttgart, 1984), pp. 467–500.
9. Seymour, M. C. *et al., Bartholomaeus Anglicus and his Encyclopedia* (Aldershot, 1992).
10. Twomey, Michael W., "Appendix: Medieval Encyclopedias," in *Medieval Christian Literary Imagery: A Guide to Interpretation,* ed. R. E. Kaske *et al.,* Toronto Medieval Bibliographies, 11 (Toronto, 1988), pp. 182–215.
11. Weijers (1991) [cf. 25.9.]
12. Zöllner, Walter, "Mittelalterliche Enzyklopädien," in *Lexika gestern und heute,* ed. Hans-Joachim Diesner and Günter Gurst (Leipzig, 1976), pp. 61–93.

27. Bilingual dictionaries (English/Latin) in the 15th century

1. Starnes (1954)★, pp. 3–37.
2. Stein (1985)★, chs 11–13.
3. *Promptorium parvulorum sive clericorum,* ed. Albert Way, 3 vols, Camden Society, 25, 54 and 89 (London, 1843–1865), III (1865), xiii–lxxxvii.
4. "The Latin–Middle English Glossary 'Medulla grammatice'," ed. Florent A. Tremblay (Ph.D. Dissertation, Catholic University of America, Washington, D.C., 1968).
5. Stein, Gabriele, "The English Dictionary in the 15th Century," in *Logos Semantikos: Studia linguistica in honorem Eugenio Coseriu 1921–1981,* ed. Horst Geckeler *et al.,* 5 vols (Berlin, 1981), I, 313–22.
6. Voigts, Linda and Frank Stubbings, "*Promptorium parvulorum:* Manuscript Fragments at Emmanuel College and their Relation to Pynson's *Editio princeps*," *Transactions of the Cambridge Bibliographical Society,* 9, part 4 (1989), 358–71.

28. Humanism and the study of language in early modern Europe

1. Arens (1969)*, pp. 62–152.
2. Robins (1990)*, ch. 5.
3. Padley (1976)*, (1985)*, (1988)*
4. Percival, W. Keith, "The Grammatical Tradition and the Rise of the Vernaculars," in Sebeok (1975)*, pp. 231–75.
5. Brekle, Herbert E., "The Seventeenth Century," in Sebeok (1975)*, pp. 277–382.
6. Aarsleff, Hans, "The Eighteenth Century, Including Leibniz," in Sebeok (1975)*, pp. 383–479.
7. Breva-Claramonte, Manuel, *Sanctius' Theory of Language: A Contribution to the History of Renaissance Linguistics,* SHLS, 27 (Amsterdam, 1983).
8. Sanctius, Franciscus, *Minerve ou les causes de la langue Latine,* introd., translation and notes by Geneviève Clerico (Lille, 1982).
9. Harnois, Guy, *Les théories du langage en France de 1660 à 1821,* Études Françaises, 2 (Paris, 1929).
10. Kukenheim, Louis, *Contributions à l'histoire de la grammaire Grecque, Latine et Hébraïque à l'époque de la Renaissance* (Leiden, 1951).
11. Michael (1970)*
12. Percival, W. Keith, "Grammar and Rhetoric in the Renaissance," in Murphy (1983) [cf. 39.13.], pp. 303–30.
13. Percival, W. Keith, "Renaissance Linguistics: The Old and the New," in Bynon-Palmer*, pp. 56–68.
14. Stéfanini, Jean, "Julius César Scaliger et son De causis linguae latinae," in Parret*, pp. 317–30.
15. Tavoni, Mirko, ed., *Renaissance Linguistics Archive 1350–1700: A First Print-Out from the Secondary-Sources Data-Base* (Ferrara, 1987). Pierre Lardet and Mirko Tavoni, eds, ... : *A Second Print-Out from the Secondary-Sources Data-Base* (Ferrara, 1988). See also Mirko Tavoni, "The 'Renaissance Linguistics Archive' Workshop at ICHoLS IV," in Dutz (1989) [cf. 4a.4.], pp. 339–43.
16. Waswo, Richard, *Language and Meaning in the Renaissance* (Princeton, N. J., 1987).

29. Humanist grammar in England; William Lily

1. Baldwin, T. W., *William Shakspere's* Small Latine & Lesse Greeke, 2 vols (Urbana, Ill., 1944).

2. Padley (1976)*, ch. 1, and (1988)*, ch. 3.

3. Shaw, A. E., "The Earliest Latin Grammars in English," *Transactions of the Bibliographical Society,* 5 (1898/1899), 39–65.

4. Watson, Foster, *The English Grammar Schools to 1660: Their Curriculum and Practice* (Cambridge, 1908), chs XIV–XVII.

5. Weiss, R., *Humanism in England during the Fifteenth Century,* third ed., Medium Aevum Monographs, 4 (Oxford, 1967), ch. XII.

6. Jensen, Kristian, "Linacre's Latin Grammar," *Journal of the Warburg and Courtauld Institutes,* 49 (1986), 106–25.

7. Lily, William, *A Shorte Introduction of Grammar,* introd. Vincent J. Flynn (repr. New York, 1945). [Reprint of the 1567 edition]

8. Blach, S., "Shakespeares Lateingrammatik: Lilys Grammatica Latina nach der ältesten bekannten Ausgabe von 1527 und der für Shakespeare in Betracht kommenden Ausgabe von 1566 (London, R. Wolfius)," *Jahrbuch der deutschen Shakespeare-Gesellschaft,* 44 (1908), 65–117, and 45 (1909), 51–100.

9. Allen, C. G., "The Sources of 'Lily's Latin Grammar': A Review of the Facts and some Further Suggestions," *The Library,* fifth ser., 9 (1954), 85–100.

10. Bennett (1969) [cf. 17.11.]

11. Flynn, Vincent Joseph, "The Grammatical Writings of William Lily, ?1468–?1523," *Papers of the Bibliographical Society of America,* 37 (1943), 85–113.

30. Linguistics and the English language: 16th to 18th centuries

1. Kennedy*, 5465–98, 12554–76. Supplemented by Rudolf Brotanek, "Englische Sprachbücher in frühneuenglischer Zeit," *ZAA,* 4 (1956), 5–18.

2. Alston*, vol. I (1965); vol. II (1967), 29–35 and 37–146; vol. III, part 1 (1970), 36–99; vol. III, part 2 (1971), 35–61.

3. Barber, Charles, *Early Modern English* (London, 1976), ch. 2.

4. Baugh-Cable*, chs 8 and 9.

5. Bergheaud, P. *et al.*, *La Réflexion linguistique en Grande-Bretagne 17ᵉ–18ᵉ siècles* (Saint-Denis, 1985) [= *Histoire, Épistémologie, Langage,* vol. 7, fasc. 11].

6. Bolton, W. F. and D. Crystal, eds., *The English Language,* 2 vols.

(Cambridge, 1966–1969), vol. I (1966): *Essays by English and American Men of Letters 1490–1839,* ed. W. F. Bolton.

7. Cohen, Murray, *Sensible Words: Linguistic Practice in England 1640– 1785* (Baltimore, 1977). [Cf. Garland Cannon, "English Grammarians of the Seventeenth and Eighteenth Centuries," *Semiotica,* 26 (1979), 121–49.]

8. Craigie, William A., *The Critique of Pure English from Caxton to Smollett,* S. P. E. Tract, 65 (Oxford, 1946).

9. Donawerth, Jane, *Shakespeare and the Sixteenth-Century Study of Language* (Urbana, Ill., 1984).

10. Gray, Douglas, "A Note on Sixteenth-Century Purism," in *Words: For Robert Burchfield's Sixty-Fifth Birthday,* ed. E. G. Stanley and T. F. Hoad (Cambridge, 1988), pp. 103–19.

11. Howatt★

12. Hüllen, Werner, *"Their Manner of Discourse": Nachdenken über Sprache im Umkreis der Royal Society* (Tübingen, 1989).

13. Johnson, Francis R., "Latin Versus English: The Sixteenth-Century Debate over Scientific Terminology," *SP,* 41 (1944), 109–35.

14. Jones (1953)★

15. McConchie, R. W., "'It hurteth memorie and hindreth learning': Attitudes to the Use of the Vernacular in Sixteenth Century English Medical Writings," *Studia Anglica Posnaniensia,* 21 (1988), 53–67.

16. McKnight★

17. Michael, Ian, *The Teaching of English: From the Sixteenth Century to 1870* (Cambridge, 1987).

18. Moore, J. L., *Tudor-Stuart Views on the Growth, Status and Destiny of the English Language,* Studien zur Englischen Philologie, 41 (Halle, 1910).

19. Nelson, William, "The Teaching of English in Tudor Grammar Schools," *SP,* 49 (1952), 119–43.

20. Padley (1985)★, chs 2.ii and 2.iii.

21. Prein, Wilhelm, *Puristische Strömungen im 16. Jahrhundert: Ein Beitrag zur englischen Sprachgeschichte* (Wanne-Eickel, 1909).

22. Rusch, Jürg, *Die Vorstellung vom Goldenen Zeitalter der englischen Sprache im 16., 17. und 18. Jahrhundert,* Schweizer Anglistische Arbeiten, 69 (Berne, 1972).

23. Salmon, Vivian, "Effort and Achievement in Seventeenth-Century British Linguistics," in Bynon-Palmer★, pp. 69–95.

24. Salmon, Vivian, *The Study of Language in 17th-Century England,* sec. rev. ed., SHLS, 17 (Amsterdam, 1988).

25. Söderlind, J., "The Attitude to Language Expressed by or Ascertainable from English Writers of the 16th and 17th Centuries," *Studia Neophilologica,* 36 (1964), 111–26.
26. Tucker, Susie I., ed., *English Examined: Two Centuries of Comment on the Mother-Tongue* (Cambridge, 1961).
27. Vos, Alvin, "Humanistic Standards of Diction in the Inkhorn Controversy," *SP,* 73 (1976), 376–96.
28. Waswo (1987) [cf. 28.16.]
29. Watson, Foster, "The Curriculum and Text-Books of English Schools in the First Half of the Seventeenth Century," *Transactions of the Bibliographical Society,* 6, II (1900–1902), 159–267.
30. *English Linguistics 1500–1800. A Collection of Facsimile Reprints,* ed. R. C. Alston, 365 vols (Menston, 1967–1972; Microfiche edition Menston, 1974). [Facsimile editions of important grammars, dictionaries and other linguistic works published mostly in England up to 1800]

31. Plans for a language academy in England and America

1. Flasdieck, H. M., *Der Gedanke einer englischen Sprachakademie in Vergangenheit und Gegenwart,* Jenaer germanistische Forschungen, 11 (Jena, 1928).
2. Funke, Otto, *Zum Weltsprachenproblem in England im 17. Jahrhundert,* Anglistische Forschungen, 69 (Heidelberg, 1929).
3. Kelly, Ann Cline, *Swift and the English Language* (Philadelphia, 1988).
4. Read, Allen Walker, "Suggestions for an Academy in England in the Latter Half of the Eighteenth Century," *Modern Philology,* 36 (1938/1939), 145–56.
5. Read, Allen Walker, "American Projects for an Academy to Regulate Speech," *PMLA,* 51 (1936), 1141–79.
6. Heath, Shirley Brice, "A National Language Academy? Debate in the New Nation," *Linguistics,* 189 (1977), 9–43.

32. English pronunciation and orthography, spelling reform: 16th to 19th centuries
— see also section 62 —

1. Kennedy★, 1117–233a, 7327–608, 7796–8016, 8094–262, 12202–316, 12755–65.
2. Alston★, vol. VI (1969), 94–118, and vol. IV (1967).

3. Dobson, E. J., *English Pronunciation 1500–1700*, sec. ed., 2 vols (Oxford, 1968).
4. Horn, Wilhelm, *Laut und Leben: Englische Lautgeschichte der neueren Zeit (1400–1950)*, rev. and ed. Martin Lehnert, 2 vols (Berlin, 1954), esp. pp. 77–116.
5. Scragg, D. G., *A History of English Spelling*, Mont Follik Series, 3 (Manchester, 1974).
6. Baron, Dennis E., *Grammar and Good Taste: Reforming the American Language* (New Haven, 1982).
7. Baugh-Cable★, §§ 156 and 231–2.
8. Bradley, Henry, "Spoken and Written English," in *The Collected Papers of Henry Bradley* (Oxford, 1928), pp. 168–93. [Originally published 1913/1914]
9. Brengelman, F. H., "Orthoepists, Printers, and the Rationalization of English Spelling," *JEGP*, 79 (1980), 332–54.
10. Craigie, William A., *Problems of Spelling Reform*, S. P. E. Tract, 63 (Oxford, 1944).
11. *DEMEP: English Pronunciation 1500–1800, Report Based on the DEMEP Symposium and Editorial Meeting at Edinburgh 23–26 October 1974*, ed. Bror Danielsson (Stockholm, 1976).
12. Dobson, E. J., "Early Modern Standard English," *TPS* (1955), 25–54.
13. Görlach, Manfred, *Introduction to Early Modern English* (Cambridge, 1991), esp. ch. 3.
14. Haas, W., ed., *Alphabets for English* (Manchester, 1969).
15. Holmberg, Börje, *On the Concept of Standard English and the History of Modern English Pronunciation*, Lunds Universitets Årsskrift, N. F. Avd. 1, vol. 56, no. 3 (Lund, 1964).
16. Abercrombie, David, D. B. Fry, P. A. D. MacCarthy, N. C. Scott and J. L. M. Trim, eds, *In Honour of Daniel Jones: Papers Contributed on the Occasion of his Eightieth Birthday 12 September 1961* (London, 1964).
17. Jespersen, Otto, *A Modern English Grammar on Historical Principles*, 7 parts, part I (Heidelberg, 1909), ch. I.
18. Jones (1953)★, ch. 5 and pp. 285–6.
19. Kabell, Inge, Hanna Lauridsen and A. Zettersten, eds, *Studies in Early Modern English Pronunciation: A DEMEP Publication*, Anglica et Americana, 20 (Copenhagen, 1984).
20. Lounsbury, Thomas R., *English Spelling and Spelling Reform* (New York, 1909).
21. McKnight★, ch. XVIII.

22. Malone, Kemp, "Benjamin Franklin on Spelling Reform," *American Speech,* 1 (1926), 96–100.

23. Mencken-McDavid*, pp. 479–502.

24. Robertson, Stuart, *The Development of Modern English,* sec. ed. rev. Frederic G. Cassidy (Englewood Cliffs, N. J., 1954), pp. 353–74.

25. Salmon, Vivian, "Wh- and Yes/No Questions: Charles Butler's *Grammar* (1633) and the History of a Linguistic Concept," in *Language Form and Linguistic Variation: Papers Dedicated to Angus McIntosh,* ed. J. Anderson, Amsterdam Studies in the Theory and History of Linguistic Science IV, 15 (Amsterdam, 1982), pp. 401–26.

26. Sheldon, Esther Keck, "Standards of English Pronunciation According to the Grammarians and Orthoepists of the 16th, 17th and 18th Centuries" (Ph. D. Dissertation, University of Wisconsin, 1938).

27. Starrett, Edmund V., *Spelling Reform Proposals for the English Language* (Detroit, 1983).

28. *John Hart's Works on English Orthography and Pronunciation (1551–1569–1570),* ed. Bror Danielsson, 2 vols, Stockholm Studies in English, 5 and 11 (Stockholm, 1955–1963).

29. *Sir Thomas Smith: Literary and Linguistic Works (1542–1549–1568),* ed. Bror Danielsson, 4 parts, Stockholm Studies in English, 12, 50 and 56 (Stockholm, 1963–); part II: *A Critical Edition of De recta et emendata linguae graecae pronuntiatione,* Stockholm Studies in English, 50 (1978), and part III: *A Critical Edition of De recta et emendata linguae anglicae scriptione, dialogus,* Stockholm Studies in English, 56 (1983). [Part IV in preparation]

30. Wallis, ed. Kemp (1972) [cf. 35.1.], "Introduction," ch. 7.

31. Pollner, Clausdirk, *Robert Nares: "Elements of Orthoepy (1784),"* Europäische Hochschulschriften, Reihe XIV: Angelsächsische Sprache und Literatur, 41 (Berne, 1976).

32. Rohlfing, Helmut, *Die Werke James Elphinstons (1721–1809) als Quellen der englischen Lautgeschichte: Eine Analyse orthoepistischer Daten,* Anglistische Forschungen, 172 (Heidelberg, 1984).

33. Salmon, Vivian, "Some Reflections of Dionysius Thrax's "Phonetics" in Sixteenth-Century English Scholarship", in V. Law, I. Sluiter, eds, *Dionysius Thrax and the Techne Grammatike* (Münster, 1995), pp. 135–50.

33. English pronouncing dictionaries

1. Kennedy★ [cf. 42.1.]
2. Alston★, vol. V (1966).
3. Abercrombie, David, *Studies in Phonetics and Linguistics,* Language and Language Learning, 10 (London, 1965), ch. 6.
4. Benzie, W., *The Dublin Orator: Thomas Sheridan's Influence on 18th-Century Rhetoric and 'Belles Lettres'* (Leeds, 1972), ch. VI.
5. Bronstein, Arthur J., "The History of Pronunciation in English-Language Dictionaries," in Hartmann (1986)★, pp. 23–33.
6. Congleton (1979) [cf. 43.8.]
7. Emsley, Bert, "James Buchanan and the Eighteenth Century Regulation of English Usage," *PMLA,* 48 (1933), 1154–66.
8. Emsley, Bert, "Progress in Pronouncing Dictionaries," *American Speech,* 15 (1940), 55–9.
9. Horn and Lehnert (1954) [cf. 32.4.], pp. 104–9.
10. McKnight★, ch. VIII.
11. Popp, Margret, *Die englische Aussprache im 18. Jahrhundert: Im Lichte englisch-französischer Zeugnisse, Teil I: Das Dictionnaire de la prononciation Angloise, 1756,* Anglistische Forschungen, 199 (Heidelberg, 1989).
12. Sheldon, Esther K., "Pronouncing Systems in Eighteenth-Century Dictionaries," *Language,* 22 (1946), 27–41.
13. Sheldon, Esther K., "Walker's Influence on the Pronunciation of English," *PMLA,* 62 (1947), 130–46.

34. English grammar: 16th to 18th centuries

1. Kennedy★, 2462–702, 5687–990a.
2. Alston★, vols I–III (1965–1970).
3. Funke, Otto, *Die Frühzeit der englischen Grammatik* (Berne, 1941).
4. Jones (1953)★
5. Michael (1970)★
6. Padley (1985)★, (1988)★
7. Poldauf, Ivan, *On the History of some Problems of English Grammar before 1800* (Prague, 1948).
8. Vorlat, Emma, *The Development of English Grammatical Theory 1586–1737: With Special Reference to the Theory of Parts of Speech* (Louvain, 1975).
9. Vorlat, Emma, *Progress in English Grammar 1585–1735: A Study of the*

Development of English Grammar and of the Interdependence among the Early English Grammarians, 4 vols (Louvain, 1963).

10. Algeo, John, "The Earliest English Grammars," in *Historical and Editorial Studies in Medieval and Early Modern English for Johan Gerritsen,* ed. Mary-Jo Arn and Hanneke Wirtjes (Groningen, 1985), pp. 191–207.

11. Enkvist, Nils Erik, "English in Latin Guise: A Note on some Renaissance Textbooks," *HL,* 2 (1975), 283–98.

12. Graband, Gerhard, *Die Entwicklung der frühneuenglischen Nominalflexion: Dargestellt vornehmlich auf Grund von Grammatikerzeugnissen des 17. Jahrhunderts* (Tübingen, 1965).

13. Horn, Jacob, *Das englische Verbum nach Zeugnissen von Grammatikern des 17. und 18. Jahrhunderts* (Diss., Giessen, 1911).

14. Joly, André, "The Study of the Article in England from Wallis to Horne Tooke 1653–1798," in Aarsleff *et al.* (1987)★, pp. 283–97.

15. Kohonen, Viljo, "On the Development of an Awareness of English Syntax in Early (1550–1660) Descriptions of Word Order by English Grammarians, Logicians and Rhetoricians," *NM,* 79 (1978), 44–58.

16. Knorrek, Marianne, *Der Einfluss des Rationalismus auf die englische Sprache: Beiträge zur Entwicklungsgeschichte der englischen Syntax im 17. und 18. Jahrhundert,* Sprache und Kultur der germanischen und romanischen Völker, Anglistische Reihe, 30 (Breslau, 1938).

17. Nagashima★, ch. 3.

18. Nelson, William, "The Teaching of English in Tudor Grammar Schools," *SP,* 49 (1952), 119–43.

19. Partridge, A. C., *Tudor to Augustan English: A Study in Syntax and Style from Caxton to Johnson* (London, 1969).

20. Robins, Robert H., "The Evolution of English Grammar Books since the Renaissance," in Leitner (1986)★, pp. 292–306.

21. Smith, Robin Deirdre, *A Syntactic Quicksand: Ellipsis in Seventeenth and Eighteenth-Century English Grammars* (Delft, 1986).

22. Sundby (1992) [cf. 38.18.]

23. Watanabe, Shoichi, *Studien zur Abhängigkeit der frühneuenglischen Grammatiken von den mittelalterlichen Lateingrammatiken* (Diss., Münster, 1958).

24. Funke, Otto, "William Bullokars *Bref Grammar for English* (1568)," *Anglia,* 62 (1938), 116–37.

25. Funke, Otto, "Ben Jonson's *English Grammar* (1640)," *Anglia,* 64 (1940), 117–34.

26. "John Evelyn's *English Grammar,*" ed. Albert B. Cook III, *Leeds Studies in English,* N. S., 15 (1984), 117–46.

27. Biletzki, Anat, "Richard Johnson: A Case of 18th-Century Prag-
matics," *HL*, 18 (1991), 281–300.

34a. Early treatments of the history of English grammar

1. Kennedy★, 5687–97, 12598–628.
2. Richardson, Charles, "English Grammar and English Grammarians,"
   The Gentleman's Magazine, 14 (1840), 365–73 and 473–81; 15 (1841),
   473–80; 16 (1841), 478–85 and 585–91.
3. Graham, G. F., "On English Grammars," *Classical Museum* (1845),
   404–10.
4. Sachs, C. E. A., "Studien zur Geschichte der englischen Grammatik,"
   Archiv, 23 (1858), 406–14.
5. Kittredge, G. L., *Some Landmarks in the History of English Grammar*
   (New York, 1903).

34b. Punctuation

1. Kennedy★, 8017–93.
2. Brown, T. Julian, "Punctuation," in *The New Encyclopaedia Britannica*,
   15th ed. (1975; rev. 1985), Macropaedia, XXIX, 1006–8.
3. Husband, Thomas F. and M. F. A. Husband, *Punctuation: Its Principles
   and Practice* (London, 1905).
4. Parkes, M. B., *Pause and Effect. An Introduction to the History of Punctuation in the West* (Aldershot, 1992).
5. Salmon, Vivian, "English Punctuation Theory 1500–1800," *Anglia*,
   106 (1988), 285–314.

35. John Wallis

1. Wallis, John, *Grammar of the English Language with an Introductory
   Grammatico-Physical Treatise on Speech (or on the Formation of all Speech
   Sounds)*, ed. and trans. J. A. Kemp (London, 1972).
2. Constantinescu, Ilinca, "John Wallis (1616–1703): A Reappraisal of his
   Contribution to the Study of English," *HL*, 1 (1974), 297–311.
3. Lehnert, Martin, *Die Grammatik des englischen Sprachmeisters John Wallis
   (1616–1703)*, Sprache und Kultur der germanischen und romanischen
   Völker, Anglistische Reihe, 21 (Breslau, 1936).
4. Padley (1985)★, ch. 2.iii.

5. Raney, George William, "The Accidence and Syntax in John Wallis' 1653 *Grammatica linguae anglicanae:* A Translation and a Commentary on its Alleged Relationship to the 1660 Port-Royal *Grammaire générale et raisonnée"* (Ph.D. Dissertation, University of Southern California, 1972).

36. Universal grammar; the Grammar of Port-Royal

1. Alston*, vol. III, part 2 (1971).
2. Padley (1976)*, chs 4 and 5; (1985)*, part 2.
3. Bergheaud, Patrice, "De James Harris à John Horne Tooke: Mutations de l'analyse du langage en Angleterre dans la deuxième moitié du XVIIIe siècle," *HL,* 6 (1979), 15–45.
4. Cohen (1977) [cf. 30.7.]
5. Funke, Otto, *Englische Sprachphilosophie im späteren 18. Jahrhundert* (Berne, 1934).
6. Funke, Otto, "Sprachphilosophie und Grammatik im Spiegel englischer Sprachbücher des 17. und 18. Jahrhunderts," *Studia Neophilologica,* 15 (1942/1943), 15–29.
7. *La Grammaire générale: Des modistes aux idéologues,* ed. André Joly and Jean Stéfanini, Publications de l'Université de Lille, 3 (Lille, 1977).
8. Michael (1970)*, esp. ch. 7.
9. Salus, Peter H., "Universal Grammar 1000–1850," in Parret*, pp. 85–101.
10. Subbiondo, Joseph L., "John Wilkin's 'Theory of Meaning' and the Development of a Semantic Model," *Cahiers linguistiques d'Ottawa,* 5 (1977), 41–61.
11. Vorlat, Emma, "Syntactic Universals in James Beattie's Theory of Language (1788)," in *Studies in Honour of René Derolez,* ed. A. M. Simon-Vandenbergen (Gent, 1987), pp. 673–83.
12. *Grammaire générale et raisonnée ou la Grammaire de Port Royal,* ed. Herbert E. Brekle (Stuttgart/Bad Cannstadt, 1966). [Cf. Robin Lakoff, *Language,* 45 (1969), 343–64.]
13. Donzé, Roland, *La Grammaire générale et raisonnée de Port-Royal: Contribution à l'histoire des idées grammaticales en France,* sec. ed. (Berne, 1971).
14. Hall, Robert A., Jr, "Some Recent Studies on Port-Royal and Vaugelas," *Acta Linguistica Hafniensia,* 12 (1969), 207–33.
15. Lakoff, Robin, "La Grammaire générale et raisonnée, ou la Grammaire de Port-Royal," in Parret*, pp. 348–73.

16. Raney (1972) [cf. 35.5.]
17. Tsiapera, Maria, and Garon Wheeler, *The Port-Royal Grammar: Sources and Influences* (Münster, 1993).

37. Universal language schemes

1. Alston*, vol. VII (1967).
2. Asbach-Schnitker, Brigitte and Hans Jürgen Höller, "Projekte zur Schaffung einer 'characteristica' und 'lingua universalis'," in Schobinger (1988) [cf. 46.18.], pp. 313–39.
3. Cohen (1977) [cf. 30.7.]
4. Cornelius, Paul, *Languages in Seventeenth- and Early Eighteenth-Century Imaginary Voyages* (Geneva, 1965).
5. Couturat, Louis and Léopold Leau, *Histoire de la langue universelle* (Paris, 1903).
6. Cram, David F., "George Dalgarno on 'Ars signorum' and Wilkins' 'Essay'," in Koerner (1980) [cf. 4a.1.], pp. 113–21.
7. Cram, David F., "Language Universals and 17th Century Universal Language Schemes," in *Rekonstruktion und Interpretation: Problemgeschichtliche Studien zur Sprachtheorie von Ockham bis Humboldt,* ed. Klaus D. Dutz and Ludger Kaczmarek, TüBL, 264 (Tübingen, 1985), pp. 243–57.
8. Funke (1929) [cf. 31.2.]
9. Hüllen (1989) [cf. 30.12.]
10. Knowlson, James, *Universal Language Schemes in England and France 1600–1800* (Toronto, 1975).
11. Large, Andrew, *The Artificial Language Movement* (Oxford, 1985).
12. Salmon (1988) [cf. 30.24.], chs 8–11.
13. Salmon, Vivian, *The Works of Francis Lodwick: A Study of his Writings in the Intellectual Context of the Seventeenth Century* (London, 1972).
14. Salmon, Vivian, "Language-Planning in Seventeenth-Century England; Its Context and Aims," in *In Memory of J. R. Firth,* ed. C. E. Bazell, J. C. Catford, M. A. K. Halliday and R. H. Robins (London, 1966), pp. 370–97.
15. Salmon, Vivian, "Nathaniel Chamberlain and his 'Tractatus de Literis et Lingua Philosophica' (1679)," in *Five Hundred Years of Words and Sounds: A Festschrift for Eric Dobson,* ed. E. G. Stanley and Douglas Gray (Cambridge, 1983), pp. 128–36.
16. Salmon, Vivian, "William Bedell and the Universal Language Move-

ment in Seventeenth-Century Ireland," *Essays and Studies*, N. S., 36 (1983), 27–39.

17. Slaughter, M. M., *Universal Languages and Scientific Taxonomy in the Seventeenth Century* (Cambridge, 1982).

18. Strasser, Gerhard F., *Lingua Universalis: Kryptologie und Theorie der Universalsprachen im 16. und 17. Jahrhundert*, Wolfenbütteler Forschungen, 38 (Wiesbaden, 1988).

19. Subbiondo, Joseph L., ed., *John Wilkins and 17th-Century British Linguistics*, SHLS, 67 (Amsterdam, 1992).

20. Yaguello, Marina, *Lunatic Lovers of Language: Imaginary Languages and Their Inventors*, trans. Catherine Slater (London, 1991).

21. Abercrombie (1965) [cf. 33.3.], ch. 6.

38. English 'prescriptive' grammar in the 18th century
— see also section 34 —

1. Leonard, Sterling Andrus, *The Doctrine of Correctness in English Usage 1700–1800,* University of Wisconsin Studies in Language and Literature, 25 (Madison, Wisconsin, 1929).

2. Austin, Frances, "Double Negatives and the Eighteenth Century," in *English Historical Linguistics,* ed. N. F. Blake and Charles Jones, CECTAL Conference Papers Series, 3 (Sheffield, 1984), pp. 138–48.

3. Baugh-Cable★, §§ 198–204.

4. Bryan, W. F., "Notes on the Founders of Prescriptive English Grammar," in *The Manly Anniversary Studies in Language and Literature* (Chicago, 1923), pp. 383–93.

5. Bryan, W. F., "A Late Eighteenth-Century Purist," *SP,* 23 (1926), 358–70.

6. Fries, Charles C., "The Rules of Common School Grammars," *PMLA,* 42 (1927), 221–37.

7. Jones, Bernard, "William Barnes on Lindley Murray's English Grammar," *ES,* 64 (1983), 30–5.

8. Knorrek (1938) [cf. 34.16.]

9. McKnight★, ch. XV.

10. Pullum, G. K., "Lowth's Grammar: A Re-Evaluation," *Linguistics,* 137 (1974), 63–78.

11. Quirk, Randolph, *The Linguist and the English Language* (London, 1974), ch. 2.

12. Read, Allen Walker, "The Motivation of Lindley Murray's Grammatical Work," *JEGP,* 38 (1939), 525–39.
13. Rogal, Samuel J., "Hurd's Editorial Criticism of Addison's Grammar and Usage," *Costerus,* N. S., 3 (1975), 13–47.
14. Subbiondo, Joseph L., "William Ward and the 'Doctrine of Correctness'," *Journal of English Linguistics,* 9 (1975), 36–46.
15. Sugg, Redding S., Jr, "The Mood of Eighteenth Century Grammar," *Philological Quarterly,* 43 (1964), 239–52.
16. Sundby, Bertil, "John Knowles on English Usage and Style," *ES,* 60 (1979), 111–21.
17. Sundby, Bertil, "Parallelism and Sequence in Early English Prescriptive Grammar," in Leitner (1986)*, pp. 397–408.
18. Sundby, Bertil, Anne Kari Bjørge and Kari E. Haugland, *A Dictionary of English Normative Grammar: 1700–1800,* SHLS, 63 (Amsterdam, 1992). [Preceded by project reports, ed. Sundby, published under the same title at Bergen, 1980–]
19. Sundby, Bertil, "A Guide to the Dictionary of English Normative Grammar," *Mediaeval English Studies Newsletter,* 19 (1988), 6–9.
20. Tucker, Susie I., *Protean Shape: A Study in Eighteenth Century Vocabulary and Usage* (London, 1967).
21. Vorlat, E., "The Sources of Lindley Murray's 'The English Grammar'," *Leuvense Bijdragen,* 48 (1959), 108–25.
22. Arnold, Roland, "*Lesser* und *Worser:* Form und Funktion bei der Entwicklung eines Typs der doppelten Steigerung," *ZAA,* 18 (1970), 283–99.

38a. *Shall* and *will*

1. Fries, Charles C., "The Periphrastic Future with *Shall* and *Will* in Modern English," *PMLA,* 40 (1925), 963–1024.
2. Hulbert, J. R., "On the Origin of the Grammarians' Rules for the Use of *Shall* and *Will*," *PMLA,* 62 (1947), 1178–82.
3. Moody, Patricia A., "*Shall* and *Will* in English Grammars: A Revised History," *HL,* 4 (1977), 281–301.
4. Taglicht, J., "The Genesis of the Conventional Rules for the Use of *Shall* and *Will*," *ES,* 51 (1970), 193–213.
5. Tieken-Boon van Ostade, Iingrid, "'I will be drowned and no man shall save me': The Conventional Rules for *Shall* and *Will* in Eighteenth-Century English Grammars," *ES,* 66 (1985), 123–42.

39. English rhetoric from the 16th century onwards

1. Kennedy★, 12772–834.
2. Alston★, vol. VI (1969).
3. Bailey, Richard W. and Dolores M. Burton, *English Stylistics: A Bibliography* (Cambridge, Mass., 1968).
4. Plett, Heinrich F., *Englische Rhetorik und Poetik 1479–1660: Eine systematische Bibliographie,* Forschungsberichte des Landes Nordrhein-Westfalen, Nr. 3201 / Fachgruppe Geisteswissenschaften (Opladen, 1985).
5. Alston, R. C. and J. L. Rosier, "Rhetoric and Style: A Bibliographical Guide," *Leeds Studies in English,* N. S., 1 (1967), 137–59.
6. Horner, Winifred Bryan, ed., *The Present State of Scholarship in Historical and Contemporary Rhetoric* (Columbia, Missouri, 1983).
7. Baldwin (1944) [cf. 29.1.], vol. II, chs XXXI–XXXVII.
8. Berdan, John M., "The Influence of the Medieval Latin Rhetorics on the English Writers of the Early Renaissance," *The Romanic Review,* 7 (1916), 288–313.
9. Howell, Wilbur Samuel, *Logic and Rhetoric in England, 1500–1700* (Princeton, N. J., 1956).
10. Howell, Wilbur Samuel, *Eighteenth Century British Logic and Rhetoric* (Princeton, N. J., 1971).
11. G. A. Kennedy (1980) [cf. 13.4.]
12. McKnight★, chs VIII and XVI.
13. Murphy, James J., ed., *Renaissance Eloquence: Studies in the Theory and Practice of Renaissance Rhetoric* (Berkeley, Calif., 1983).
14. Sandford, William P., "English Rhetoric Reverts to Classicism, 1600–1650," *The Quarterly Journal of Speech,* 15 (1929), 503–25.
15. Schäfer, Jürgen, "Elizabethan Rhetorical Terminology and Historical Lexicography," *Dictionaries,* 3 (1980/1981), 7–17.
16. Sonnino, Lee A., *A Handbook to Sixteenth-Century Rhetoric* (London, 1968).
17. Vickers, Brian, *Classical Rhetoric in English Poetry* (London, 1970).
18. *The Rhetoric of Blair, Campbell, and Whately,* ed. James L. Golden and Edward P. J. Corbett (New York, 1968).
19. Blair, Hugh, *Lectures on Rhetoric and Belles Lettres,* ed. Harold F. Harding, 2 vols (Carbondale, Ill., 1965).
20. Campbell, George, *The Philosophy of Rhetoric,* ed. with a critical intro. Lloyd F. Bitzer (Carbondale, Ill., 1963).

21. Bryan, W. F., "A Late Eighteenth-Century Purist," *SP*, 23 (1926), 358–70.
22. Frank, Thomas, "Linguistic Theory and the Doctrine of Usage in George Campbell's *Philosophy of Rhetoric*," *Lingua e Stile*, 20 (1985), 199–216.

40. English bilingual lexicography, 16th to 19th centuries

— General and Latin —

1. Kennedy*, 2733–923.
2. Stein (1985)*
3. Hartmann (1986)*
4. Starnes (1954)*
5. Starnes, DeWitt T., *Robert Estienne's Influence on Lexicography* (Austin, Texas, 1963).
6. Mayor, J. E. B., "Latin-English Lexicography," continued as "Latin-English and English-Latin Lexicography," *Journal of Classical and Sacred Philology*, 2 (1855), 271–90, and 4 (1857), 1–44.
7. F. Watson (1908) [cf. 29.4.], ch. XXIII.
8. Stein, Gabriele, "Peter Levins: A Sixteenth-Century English Word-Formationalist," in *Neuere Forschungen zur Wortbildung und Historiographie der Linguistik: Festgabe für Herbert E. Brekle zum 50. Geburtstag*, ed. Brigitte Asbach-Schnitker and Johannes Roggenhofer, TüBL, 284 (Tübingen, 1987), pp. 287–302.

— French —

9. Anderson, James David, *The Development of the English-French, French-English Bilingual Dictionary: A Study in Comparative Lexicography*, Supplement to *Word*, vol. 28, no. 3, Dec. 1972 = Monograph, no. 6 (London, 1978).
10. Bately, Janet, "Miège and the Development of the English Dictionary," in *Five Hundred Years of Words and Sounds: A Festschrift for Eric Dobson*, ed. E. G. Stanley and Douglas Gray (Cambridge, 1983), pp. 1–10.
11. Hausmann, Franz Josef, "La lexicographie bilingue anglais-français, français-anglais," in *WDD**, vol. III, sect. 309.
12. Kibbee, Douglas A., "Bilingual Lexicography in the Renaissance: Palsgrave's English-French Lexicon (1530)," in Aarsleff et al. (1987)*, pp. 179–88.
13. Kibbee (1991) [cf. 18.5.]

14. Smalley, Vera E., *The Sources of* A Dictionarie of the French and English Tongues *by Randle Cotgrave (London, 1611): A Study in Renaissance Lexicography,* The Johns Hopkins Studies in Romance Literatures and Languages, Extra Volume, 25 (Baltimore, 1948).

15. Stein, Gabriele, "Reference Point and Authorial Involvement in John Palsgrave's *Esclarcissement de la langue francoyse,*" in *Perspectives on Language in Performance: Studies in Linguistics, Literary Criticism and Language Teaching and Learning to Honour Werner Hüllen on the Occasion of his Sixtieth Birthday,* ed. Wolfgang Lörscher and Rainer Schulze, TüBL, 317 (Tübingen, 1987), pp. 530–46.

— Italian —

16. O'Connor, Desmond, "Bilingual Lexicography: English-Italian, Italian-English," in *WDD*★, vol. III, sect. 311.

17. O'Connor, D. J., "John Florio's Contribution to Italian-English Lexicography," *Italica,* 49 (1972), 49–67.

18. Rosier, James L., "Lexical Strata in Florio's *New World of Words,*" *ES,* 44 (1963), 415–23.

— Spanish —

19. Steiner, Roger J., *Two Centuries of Spanish and English Bilingual Lexicography (1590–1800),* JL, Series Practica, 108 (The Hague, 1970).

20. Steiner, Roger J., "The Three-Century Recension in Spanish and English Lexicography," in Hartmann (1986)★, pp. 229–39.

21. Steiner, Roger Jacob, "Bilingual Lexicography: English-Spanish and Spanish-English," in *WDD*★, vol. III, sect. 308.

— Dutch and German —

22. Osselton, N. E., *The Dumb Linguists: A Study of the Earliest English and Dutch Dictionaries,* Publications of the Sir Thomas Browne Institute Leiden, Special Series, 5 (Leiden, 1973).

23. Stein, Gabriele, "English-German / German-English Lexicography: Its Early Beginnings," *Lexicographica,* 1 (1985), 134–64.

24. Hausmann, Franz-Josef and Margaret Cop, "Short History of English-German Lexicography," in *Symposium on Lexicography II: Proceedings of the Second International Symposium on Lexicography May 16–17, 1984, at the University of Copenhagen,* ed. Karl Hyldgaard-Jensen and Arne Zettersten, Lexicographica, Series Maior, 5 (Tübingen, 1985), pp. 183–97.

25. Flügel, F. A., "Die englische Lexikographie in Deutschland seit Adelung (1783)," *Archiv,* 8 (1851), 250–90.

41. Polyglot dictionaries

1. Kennedy★, 2711–32.
2. Alston★, vol. II (1967), 1–28.
3. Stein (1985)★
4. Stein, Gabriele, "Sixteenth-Century English-Vernacular Dictionaries," in Hartmann (1986)★, pp. 219–28.
5. Stein (1985) [cf. 40.23.]
6. Stein, Gabriele, "The Emerging Role of English in the Dictionaries of Renaissance Europe," *Folia Linguistica Historica*, 9 (1990), 29–138.
7. Schäfer, Jürgen, "Introduction" to John Minsheu, *Ductor in Linguas (Guide into the Tongues) and Vocabularium Hispanicolatinum (A Most Copious Spanish Dictionary) (1617)*, Scholar's Facsimiles and Reprints, 321 (Delmar, New York, 1978).

42. Monolingual dictionaries and glossaries of English, 16th to 19th centuries
— see also section 69a —

1. Kennedy★, 6158–704, 12629–754.
2. Alston★, vols III (1970/1971) and V (1966).
3. O'Neill, Robert Keating, *English-Language Dictionaries, 1604–1900. The Catalog of the Warren N. and Suzanne B. Cordell Collection* (New York, 1988).
4. Schäfer, Jürgen, *Early Modern English Lexicography*, 2 vols (Oxford, 1989).
5. Hulbert, James Root, *Dictionaries: British and American*, sec. ed. (London, 1968).
6. Lehnert, Martin, "Das englische Wörterbuch in Vergangenheit und Gegenwart," *ZAA*, 4 (1956), 265–323.
7. Mathews, Mitford M., *A Survey of English Dictionaries* (London, 1933).
8. Murray, James A. H., *The Evolution of English Lexicography*, The Romanes Lecture 1900 (Oxford, 1900).
9. Osselton, Noel Edward, "English Lexicography from the Beginning up to and Including Johnson," in *WDD*★, vol. II, sect. 197.
10. Starnes-Noyes★ [with bibliography by Gabriele Stein]
11. Simpson, John A., "English Lexicography after Johnson to 1945," in *WDD*★, vol. II, sect. 198.
12. Bately, Janet M., "Ray, Worlidge and Kersey's Revision of *The New World of English Words*," *Anglia*, 85 (1967), 1–14.

13. Bately, Janet, "The Old, the New and the Strange: On some Dictionaries from the Reign of William and Mary (1688–1702)," in *Words: For Robert Burchfield's Sixty-Fifth Birthday,* ed. E. G. Stanley and T. F. Hoad (Cambridge, 1988), pp. 9–36.

14. Dolezal, Fredric, *Forgotten but Important Lexicographers: John Wilkins and William Lloyd. A Modern Approach to Lexicography before Johnson,* Lexicographica, Series Maior, 4 (Tübingen, 1985).

15. Graband, Gerhard, "Die frühne. Tradition der 'Hard Words' und der *Vindex Anglicus* (1644)," *NM,* 76 (1975), 88–107.

16. Hayashi, Tetsuro, *The Theory of English Lexicography 1530–1791,* SHLS, 18 (Amsterdam, 1978). [Review by H. Käsmann, *Anglia,* 100 (1982), 160–2.]

17. Hupka, Werner, *Wort und Bild: Die Illustrationen in Wörterbüchern und Enzyklopädien,* Lexicographica, Series Maior, 22 (Tübingen, 1989).

18. Jones (1953)★, pp. 272–7.

19. Kerling, Johan, "English Old-Word Glossaries 1553–1594," *Neophilologus,* 63 (1979), 136–47.

20. Landau, Sidney I., *Dictionaries: The Art and Craft of Lexicography* (New York, 1984), ch. 2.

21. Osselton, Noel E., *Branded Words in English Dictionaries before Johnson,* Groningen Studies in English, 7 (Groningen, 1958).

22. Osselton, Noel E., "John Kersey and the Ordinary Words of English," *ES,* 60 (1979), 555–61.

23. Osselton, Noel E., "The First English Dictionary? A Sixteenth-Century Compiler at Work," in Hartmann (1986)★, pp. 175–84.

24. Read, Allen Walker, "Projected English Dictionaries, 1755–1828," *JEGP,* 36 (1937), 188–205 and 347–66.

25. Riddell, James A., "The Beginning: English Dictionaries of the First Half of the Seventeenth Century," *Leeds Studies in English,* N. S., 7 (1974), 117–53.

26. Riddell, James A., "Some Additional Sources for Early English Dictionaries," *The Huntington Library Quarterly,* 46 (1983), 223–35.

27. Schäfer, Jürgen, "The Hard Word Dictionaries: A Re-Assessment," *Leeds Studies in English,* N. S., 4 (1970), 31–48.

28. Schäfer, Jürgen, "The Working Methods of Thomas Blount," *ES,* 59 (1978), 405–8.

29. Schäfer, Jürgen, "Glossar, Index, Wörterbuch und Enzyklopädie: Der Beginn einsprachiger Lexikographie zur Zeit Shakespeares," in *Theoretische und praktische Probleme der Lexikographie: 1. Augsburger Kolloquium,*

ed. Dieter Goetz and Thomas Herbst (Munich, 1984), pp. 276–99.

30. Wells, Ronald A., *Dictionaries and the Authoritarian Tradition: A Study in English Usage and Lexicography,* JL, Series Practica, 196 (The Hague, 1973).

42a. Early treatments of the history of English lexicography

1. Worcester, Joseph E., *A Dictionary of the English Language* (Boston, 1860), pp. liii–lxv.
2. Wheatley, Henry B., "Chronological Notices of the Dictionaries of the English Language," *TPS* (1865), 218–93. [Wheatley's chronological list, pp. 288–91, was reprinted, together with additions, by W. W. Skeat in *English Dialect Society,* no. 2, ed. Walter W. Skeat and J. H. Nodal (London, 1873), pp. 3–11.]
3. Long, Percy W., "English Dictionaries before Webster," *Papers of the Bibliographical Society of America,* 4 (1909), 25–43.

42b. Substandard English: early dictionaries and treatments

1. Kennedy★, 11868–2020, 12042–75, 12352–410.
2. Alston★, vol. IX (1971).
3. Burke, W. J., *The Literature of Slang* (New York, 1939).
4. Starnes-Noyes★, Appendix II.
5. Partridge, Eric, *Slang To-day and Yesterday: With a Short Historical Sketch; and Vocabularies of English, American and Australian Slang,* fourth ed. (London, 1970).

43. Dr. Johnson's *Dictionary*

1. Congleton, James Edmund and Elizabeth Congleton, *Johnson's Dictionary: Bibliographical Survey 1746–1984 with Excerpts for all Entries* (Terre Haute, Ind., 1984). [Not complete]
2. Courtney, William Prideaux and David Nichol Smith, *A Bibliography of Samuel Johnson* (Oxford, 1915), pp. 39–72.
3. Chapman, R. W., *Johnsonian Bibliography. A Supplement to Courtney* (Oxford, 1939).
4. Alston★, vol. V (1966).
5. Clifford, James L. and Donald J. Greene, *Samuel Johnson: A Survey and*

Bibliography of Critical Studies (Minneapolis, Minnesota, 1970), pp. 213–25.

6. Kolb, Gwin J., "Studies of Johnson's Dictionary 1956–1990," *Dictionaries,* 12 (1990), 113–26.

7. Allen, Harold Byron, "Samuel Johnson and the Authoritarian Principle in Linguistic Criticism" (Ph. D. Dissertation, University of Michigan, 1941).

8. Congleton, J. E., "Pronunciation in Johnson's Dictionary," in *Papers on Lexicography in Honor of Warren N. Cordell,* ed. J. E. Congleton, J. Edward Gates and Donald Hobar (Terre Haute, Ind., 1979), pp. 59–81.

9. Gross, Jeffrey T., "Dr. Johnson's Treatment of English Particles in the *Dictionary,*" *University of Mississippi Studies in English,* N. S., 2 (1981), 71–92.

10. McLaverty, James, "From Definition to Explanation: Locke's Influence on Johnson's Dictionary," *Journal of the History of Ideas,* 47 (1986), 377–94.

11. DeMaria, Robert, Jr, "The Theory of Language in Johnson's *Dictionary,*" in *Johnson after Two Hundred Years,* ed. Paul J. Korshin (Philadelphia, 1986), pp. 159–74.

12. DeMaria, Robert, Jr, *Johnson's* Dictionary *and the Language of Learning* (Oxford, 1986).

13. Nagashima★

14. Reddick, Allen, *The Making of Johnson's Dictionary 1746–1773* (Cambridge, 1990).

15. Schreyer, Rüdiger, *Untersuchungen zur Sprachauffassung Dr. Johnsons* (Diss., Saarbrücken, 1971).

16. Sledd, James H. and Gwin J. Kolb, eds, *Dr. Johnson's Dictionary: Essays in the Biography of a Book* (Chicago, 1955).

17. Stein, Gabriele, "Word-Formation in Dr. Johnson's Dictionary of the English Language," *Dictionaries,* 6 (1984), 66–112.

18. Wales, Kathleen, "Johnson's Use of Synonyms in *Dictionary* and Prose Style: The Influence of John Locke?," *Prose Studies,* 8,1 (1985), 25–34.

19. Weinbrot, Howard D., "Samuel Johnson's *Plan* and Preface to the *Dictionary:* The Growth of a Lexicographer's Mind," in *New Aspects of Lexicography: Literary Criticism, Intellectual History, and Social Change,* ed. Howard D. Weinbrot (Carbondale, Ill., 1972), pp. 73–94.

20. Wimsatt, W. K., Jr, "Johnson's Dictionary," in *New Light on Dr Johnson: Essays on the Occasion of his 250th Birthday,* ed. Frederick W. Hilles (New Haven, 1959), pp. 65–90.

21. Horgan, A. D., *Johnson on Language. An Introduction* (London, 1994).

44. English encyclopedias

1. Alston*, vol. III, part 1 (1970).
2. Walsh, S. Padraig [James Patrick], *Anglo-American General Encyclopedias: A Historical Bibliography 1703–1967* (New York, 1968).
3. Kafker, Frank A., ed., *Notable Encyclopedias of the Seventeenth and Eighteenth Centuries: Nine Predecessors of the Encyclopédie,* Studies on Voltaire and the Eighteenth Century, 194 (Oxford, 1981).
4. Collison (1966) [cf. 26.4.]
5. Collison, Robert L. and Warren E. Preece, "Encyclopaedias," in *The New Encyclopaedia Britannica,* 15th ed. (1975; rev. 1985), Macropaedia, XVIII, 366–85.

45. Dictionaries of English synonyms

1. Kennedy*, 9731–881.
2. Alston*, vol. III, part 1 (1970).
3. Egan, Rose F., "Survey of the History of English Synonymy," in *Webster's Dictionary of Synonyms* (Springfield, Mass., 1942), pp. vii–xxviii, and *Webster's New Dictionary of Synonyms* (Springfield, Mass., 1968), pp. 5a–23a.
4. Hausmann, Franz Josef, "The Dictionary of Synonyms: Discriminating Synonymy," in *WDD*, vol. II, sect. 102.
5. Noyes, Gertrude E., "The Beginnings of the Study of Synonyms in England," *PMLA,* 66 (1951), 951–70.
6. Kirkpatrick, Betty, "Dr Peter Mark Roget and his Thesaurus," in *Roget's Thesaurus of English Words and Phrases,* newly ed. Betty Kirkpatrick (London, 1987), pp. ix–xv. [*Ibid.,* pp. xvii–xxix: Roget's "Preface" and "Introduction" to the original edition of 1852]

46. Linguistics in England, 16th to 18th centuries: special fields

1. Alston*, vol. III, part 2 (1971), and vol. VII (1967).
2. Salmon (1986) [cf. 30.23.]
3. Salmon, Vivian, "Anglo-Dutch Linguistic Scholarship: A Survey of Seventeenth-Century Achievements," *HL,* 15 (1988), 129–53.
   — Origin of language, language typology —
4. Borst, Arno, *Der Turmbau von Babel: Geschichte der Meinungen über*

Ursprung und Vielfalt der Sprachen und Völker, 4 parts, 6 vols (Stuttgart, 1957–1963).

5. Coseriu, Eugenio, "Adam Smith and the Beginnings of Language Typology," *HL,* 10 (1983), 1–12.

6. Gessinger, Joachim and Wolfert von Rahden, eds, *Theorien vom Ursprung der Sprache,* 2 vols (Berlin, 1989).

7. Hewes, Gordon Winant, *Language Origins: A Bibliography,* sec. ed., 2 vols, Approaches to Semiotics, 44 (The Hague, 1975).

8. Stam, James H., *Inquiries into the Origin of Language: The Fate of a Question* (New York, 1976).

9. Vorlat, Emma, "The Origin and Development of Language According to Monboddo," in *Essays towards a History of Semantics,* ed. Peter Schmitter (Münster, 1990), pp. 83–103.

     — Philosophy of language —

10. Aarsleff, Hans, *From Locke to Saussure: Essays on the Study of Language and Intellectual History* (London, 1982).

11. Brekle (1975) [cf. 28.5.]

12. Coseriu, Eugenio, *Die Geschichte der Sprachphilosophie von der Antike bis zur Gegenwart: Eine Übersicht,* 2 vols, TüBL, 11 and 28 (Tübingen, I: sec. ed. 1975, II: 1972).

13. Formigari, Lia, *Language and Experience in 17th-Century British Philosophy,* SHLS, 48 (Amsterdam, 1988).

14. Funke, Otto, "Sprachphilosophische Probleme bei Bacon," *Englische Studien,* 61 (1926/1927), 24–56.

15. Funke, Otto, *Studien zur Geschichte der Sprachphilosophie* (Berne, 1928).

16. Funke (1934) [cf. 36.5.]

17. Land, Stephen K., *The Philosophy of Language in Britain: Major Theories from Hobbes to Thomas Reid,* AMS Studies in the Seventeenth Century, 2 (New York, 1986).

18. *Die Philosophie des 17. Jahrhunderts,* vol. III: *England,* ed. Jean-Pierre Schobinger, 2 Halbbände, Grundriss der Geschichte der Philosophie, begründet von Friedrich Überweg (Basel, 1988).

19. Rauter, Herbert, *Die Sprachauffassung der englischen Vorromantik in ihrer Bedeutung für die Literaturkritik und Dichtungstheorie der Zeit* (Bad Homburg v.d. H., 1970).

     — Language teaching, language learning —

20. Alston*, vols II (1967) and X (1972).

21. Kennedy*, 13049–53.

22. Howatt*

23. Kelly, Louis G., *25 Centuries of Language Teaching* (Rowley, Mass., 1969).
24. Lawson, John and Harold Silver, *A Social History of Education in England* (London, 1973).
25. Michael (1987) [cf. 30.17.]
26. Salmon, Vivian, "The Study of Foreign Languages in Seventeenth-Century England," in Bergheaud *et al.* (1985) [cf. 30.5.], 45–70.

— Shorthand —

27. Alston★, vol. VIII (1966).
28. Butler, Edward H., *The Story of British Shorthand* (London, 1951).
29. Friedrich, Paul E., "Studien zur englischen Stenographie im Zeitalter Shakespeares: Timothe Brights Characterie entwicklungsgeschichtlich und kritisch betrachtet," *Archiv für Schriftkunde*, 1,3 and 1,4 (1915/1916), 88–140 and 147–88.
30. Johnen, Christian, *Allgemeine Geschichte der Kurzschrift*, fourth ed. (Berlin, 1940).
31. Kökeritz, Helge, "English Pronunciation as Described in Shorthand Systems of the 17th and 18th Centuries," *Studia Neophilologica*, 7 (1934/1935), 73–146.
32. Matthews, W., *English Pronunciation and Shorthand in the Early Modern Period*, University of California Publications in English, 9, no. 3 (Berkeley, Calif., 1943).

47. English and its grammar in the 19th century

1. Kennedy★, 5991–6134.
2. Dekeyser, Xavier, *Number and Case Relations in 19th Century British English: A Comparative Study of Grammar and Usage* (Antwerpen, 1975).
3. Leitner, Gerhard, "English Traditional Grammars in the Nineteenth Century," in *Linguistics Across Historical and Geographical Boundaries: In Honour of Jacek Fisiak on the Occasion of his Fiftieth Birthday,* ed. Dieter Kastovsky and Aleksander Szwedek, 2 vols, Trends in Linguistics, Studies and Monographs, 32 (Berlin, 1986), pp. 1333–55.
4. Leitner (1986)★ and Leitner (1991)★
5. McKnight★, ch. XX.
6. Aarts, F. G. A. M., "William Cobbett: Radical Reactionary and Poor Man's Grammarian," *Neophilologus,* 70 (1986), 603–14.
7. Baron (1982) [cf. 32.6.]
8. Drake, Glendon F., *The Role of Prescriptivism in American Linguistics 1820–1970,* SHLS, 13 (Amsterdam, 1977).

9. Lyman, Rollo L., *English Grammar in American Schools before 1850* (Washington, D. C., 1922).

10. Tyler, Priscilla, "Grammars of the English Language to 1850: With Special Emphasis on School Grammars Used in America" (Ph.D. Dissertation, Western Reserve University, 1953).

11. Michael (1987) [cf. 30.17.]

12. Howatt*, part III.

48. Historical and comparative linguistics in the 19th century

1. Arens (1969)*, pp. 155–399.

2. Robins (1990)*, ch. 7.

3. Amsterdamska, Olga, *Schools of Thought: The Development of Linguistics from Bopp to Saussure,* Sociology of the Sciences Monographs, 6 (Dordrecht, 1987).

4. Christmann, Hans Helmut, ed., *Sprachwissenschaft des 19. Jahrhunderts,* Wege der Forschung, 474 (Darmstadt, 1977).

5. Delbrück, Berthold, *Einleitung in das Studium der indogermanischen Sprachen: Ein Beitrag zur Geschichte und Methodik der vergleichenden Sprachforschung,* sixth ed. (Leipzig, 1919).

6. Fries, Charles C., "Linguistics: The Study of Language," in *Linguistics and Reading* (New York, 1963), ch. II.

7. Gipper, Helmut and Peter Schmitter, *Sprachwissenschaft und Sprachphilosophie im Zeitalter der Romantik,* sec. ed., TüBL, 123 (Tübingen, 1985).

8. Ivić (1965) [cf. 4.10.], chs 6–12.

9. Jankowsky, Kurt R., *The Neogrammarians: A Re-Evaluation of their Place in the Development of Linguistic Science,* JL, Series Minor, 116 (The Hague, 1972).

10. Jespersen, Otto, "History of Linguistic Science," in *Language: Its Nature, Development and Origin* (London, 1922), pp. 19–99.

11. Lehmann, Winfred P., *A Reader in Nineteenth-Century Historical Indo-European Linguistics,* Indiana University Studies in the History and Theory of Linguistics (Bloomington, Ind., 1967).

12. Morpurgo Davies, Anna, "Language Classification in the Nineteenth Century," in Sebeok (1975)*, pp. 607–716.

13. Pedersen, Holger, *Linguistic Science in the 19th Century,* trans. John Webster Spargo (Cambridge, Mass., 1931). [Reprinted as *The Discovery*

of Language: Linguistic Science in the 19th Century (Bloomington, Ind., 1962). Original ed. in Danish, 1924]

14. *TPS* (1978): *Commemorative Volume: The Neogrammarians.*
15. Wilbur, Terence H., ed., *The Lautgesetz Controversy: A Documentation,* newly ed. E. F. K. Koerner, Amsterdam Studies in the Theory and History of Linguistic Science I, 9 (Amsterdam, 1977).
16. Robins, R. H., "The Life and Work of Sir William Jones," *TPS* (1987), 1–23.
17. Cannon, Garland, *The Life and Mind of Oriental Jones. Sir William Jones, the Father of Modern Linguistics* (Cambridge, 1990).
18. Diderichsen, Paul, *Ganzheit und Struktur: Ausgewählte sprachwissenschaftliche Abhandlungen,* Internationale Bibliothek für allgemeine Linguistik, 30 (Munich, 1976).
19. Hoenigswald, Henry M., ed., *The European Background of American Linguistics: Papers of the Third Golden Anniversary Symposium of the Linguistic Society of America* (Dordrecht, 1979).
20. Hoenigswald, Henry M., "Nineteenth-Century Linguistics on Itself," in Bynon-Palmer★, pp. 172–88.
21. Hoenigswald, Henry M., "The *Annus Mirabilis* 1876 and Posterity," *TPS* (1978), 17–35.
22. Morpurgo Davies, Anna, "Karl Brugmann and Late Nineteenth-Century Linguistics," in Bynon-Palmer★, pp. 150–71.
23. Schneider, Gisela, *Zum Begriff des Lautgesetzes in der Sprachwissenschaft seit den Junggrammatikern,* TüBL, 46 (Tübingen, 1973).

49. Early forerunners of historical and comparative linguistics

1. Beyer★, ch. 2.
2. Bonfante, Giuliano, "Ideas on Kinship of the European Languages from 1200 to 1800," *Cahiers d'histoire mondiale / Journal of World History,* 1 (1953/1954), 679–99.
3. Borst (1957–1963) [cf. 46.4.]
4. Coseriu (1983) [cf. 46.5.]
5. Droixhe, Daniel, *La linguistique et l'appel de l'histoire (1600–1800): Rationalisme et révolutions positivistes,* Langue et cultures, 10 (Geneva, 1978).
6. Eros, John F., "A 17th-Century Demonstration of Language Relationship: Meric Casaubon on English and Greek," *HL,* 3 (1976), 1–15.

7. Gneuss, Helmut, "Giraldus Cambrensis und die Geschichte der englischen Sprachwissenschaft im Mittelalter," in *Language and Civilization: A Concerted Profusion of Essays and Studies in Honour of Otto Hietsch,* ed. Claudia Blank *et al.,* 2 vols (Frankfurt/Main, 1992), I, 164–72.

8. Metcalf, George J., "The Indo-European Hypothesis in the Sixteenth and Seventeenth Centuries," in Hymes (1975) [cf. 4a.9.], pp. 233–57.

50. The study of Old English since the later 16th century

1. Kennedy*, 3120–306.

2. Alston*, vol. III, part 1 (1970).

3. Greenfield, Stanley B. and Fred C. Robinson, *A Bibliography of Publications on Old English Literature to the End of 1972* (Toronto, 1980), nos 801A–72 and *passim.*

4. Wülker, Richard, *Grundriss zur Geschichte der angelsächsischen Litteratur* (Leipzig, 1885).

5. Adams, Eleanor N., *Old English Scholarship in England from 1566–1800,* Yale Studies in English, 55 (New Haven, 1917).

6. Bennett, J. A. W., "The History of Old English and Old Norse Studies in England from the Time of Francis Junius till the End of the Eighteenth Century" (D. Phil. Dissertation, Oxford, 1938).

7. Bennett, J. A. W., *The Humane Medievalist and Other Essays in English Literature and Learning from Chaucer to Eliot,* ed. Piero Boitani (Rome, 1982), chs IX and X. ["The Oxford Saxonists"; "Hickes's *Thesaurus*"]

8. Berkhout, Carl T. and Milton McC. Gatch, eds, *Anglo-Saxon Scholarship: The First Three Centuries* (Boston, Mass., 1982). [Cf. the review by Angelika Lutz, *Anglia,* 101 (1983), 480–7.]

9. Douglas, David C., *English Scholars 1660–1730,* sec. ed. (London, 1951).

10. Fairer, David, "Anglo-Saxon Studies," in *The History of the University of Oxford,* vol. V: *The Eighteenth Century,* ed. L. S. Sutherland and L. G. Mitchell (Oxford, 1986), pp. 807–29.

11. Frantzen, Allen J., *Desire for Origins: New Language, Old English and Teaching the Tradition* (New Brunswick, 1990).

12. Harris, Richard L., ed., *A Chorus of Grammars: The Correspondence of George Hickes and his Collaborators on the* Thesaurus linguarum septentrionalium (Toronto, 1992).

13. Hetherington, M. S., *The Beginnings of Old English Lexicography,* (privately printed, 1980). [See also Bailey (1990), 55.3.]

14. Jones (1953)*, chs VII–VIII.
15. Lutz, Angelika, "Zur Entstehungsgeschichte von William Somners *Dictionarium Saxonico-Latino-Anglicum,*" *Anglia,* 106 (1988), 1–25.
16. Stanley, E. G., "The Scholarly Recovery of the Significance of Anglo-Saxon Records in Prose and Verse: A New Bibliography," *ASE,* 9 (1981), 223–62.

51. The beginnings of English palaeography

1. Kennedy*, 2008–71; 2072–153 [Runes].
2. Bischoff, Bernhard, *Latin Palaeography: Antiquity and the Middle Ages,* trans. Dáibhí Ó Cróinín and David Ganz (Cambridge, 1990), pp. 1–3.
3. Denholm-Young, N., *Handwriting in England and Wales,* sec. ed. (Cardiff, 1964).
4. Foerster, Hans, *Abriss der lateinischen Paläographie,* sec. ed. (Stuttgart, 1963), pp. 9–36.
5. Stiennon, Jacques, *Paléographie du Moyen Age* (Paris, 1973), chs I,1.–6.
6. Traube, Ludwig, *Vorlesungen und Abhandlungen,* ed. Franz Boll, Paul Lehmann, Samuel Brandt, 3 vols (Munich, 1909–1920).
7. Sisam, Kenneth, "Humfrey Wanley," in *Studies in the History of Old English Literature* (Oxford, 1953), pp. 259–77.
8. Wright, C. E., "Humfrey Wanley: Saxonist and Library-Keeper," Sir Israel Gollancz Memorial Lecture, *Proceedings of the British Academy,* 46 (1960), 99–129.
9. *Letters of Humfrey Wanley: Palaeographer, Anglo-Saxonist, Librarian 1672–1726,* ed. P. L. Heyworth (Oxford, 1989).

52. Middle English and Chaucer's language: before the 19th century

1. Kennedy*, 4318–68.
2. Alston*, vol. III, part 1 (1970).
3. Hammond, Eleanor Prescott, *Chaucer: A Bibliographical Manual* (New York, 1908), pp. 504–9.
4. Kerling (1979) [cf. 42.19.]
5. Kerling, Johan, *Chaucer in Early English Dictionaries: The Old-Word Tradition in English Lexicography down to 1721 and Speght's Chaucer Glossaries,* Germanic and Anglistic Studies of the University of Leiden, 18 (The Hague, 1979).

6. Kerling, Johan, "Franciscus Junius, 17th-Century Lexicography and Middle English," in *LEXeter '83 Proceedings: Papers from the International Conference on Lexicography at Exeter, 9–12 September 1983,* ed. R. R. K. Hartmann, Lexicographica, Series Maior, 1 (Tübingen, 1984), pp. 92–100.

7. Schäfer, Jürgen, "Chaucer in Shakespeare's Dictionaries: The Beginning," *The Chaucer Review,* 17 (1982/1983), 182–92.

8. Schäfer, Jürgen, "Alt- und Mittelenglisch in der lexikographischen Tradition des 17. Jahrhunderts," in *Festschrift für Karl Schneider zum 70. Geburtstag am 18. April 1982,* ed. Ernst S. Dick and Kurt R. Jankowsky (Amsterdam, 1982), pp. 169–85.

9. Schäfer, Jürgen, "Tod und Winterschlaf in der lexikographischen Tradition: Ein Problem moderner Lexikographie," *Anglistentag 1981: Vorträge,* ed. Jörg Hasler, Trierer Studien zur Literatur, 7 (Frankfurt/Main, 1983), pp. 35–44.

10. Wright, H. G., "Thomas Speght as a Lexicographer and Annotator of Chaucer's Works," *ES,* 40 (1959), 194–208.

53. Thomas Chatterton

1. Alston★, vol. III, part 1 (1970).

2. Warren, Murray, *A Descriptive and Annotated Bibliography of Thomas Chatterton* (New York, 1977).

3. *The Complete Works of Thomas Chatterton: A Bicentenary Edition,* ed. Donald S. Taylor and Benjamin B. Hoover, 2 vols (Oxford, 1971).

4. *The Rowley Poems by Thomas Chatterton; Reprinted from Tyrwhitt's Third Edition,* ed. Maurice Evan Hare (Oxford, 1911). [Pp. 309–33: Tyrwhitt's Appendix on the language of the Rowley Poems]

5. *The Poetical Works of Thomas Chatterton,* ed. Walter W. Skeat, 2 vols (London, 1871). [II, vii–xlvi: Skeat's "Essay on the Rowley Poems"]

54. Early treatments of the history of English

1. Kennedy★, 329ff., 12458–553.

2. Beyer★

3. Nagashima★, ch. II.

4. Tucker (1961) [cf. 30.26.]

5. Salmon (1986) [cf. 30.23.]

6. Camden, William, *Remains Concerning Britain,* ed. R. D. Dunn (Toronto, 1984), pp. 22–36.

7. Goepp, Philip H., II, "Verstegan's 'Most Ancient Saxon Words'," in *Philologica: The Malone Anniversary Studies,* ed. Thomas A. Kirby and Henry Bosley Woolf (Baltimore, 1949), pp. 249–55.
8. Gilmore, Thomas B., Jr, "Johnson's Attitudes toward French Influence on the English Language," *Modern Philology,* 78 (1980/1981), 243–60.
9. Spoerl, Karin, "Geschichtsschreibung der englischen Sprache" (unpublished Examination Thesis, Munich University, 1986).

55. Etymology, etymological and historical dictionaries of English up to the 19th century
— see also section 16 —

1. Kennedy★, 1234ff., 8385–435, 13365–80.
2. Alston★, vol. V (1966), 68–9.
3. Bailey, Richard W., "The Period Dictionary III: English," in *WDD★,* vol. II, sect. 155.
4. Schäfer, Jürgen, "Das etymologische Bewusstsein der Shakespeare-Zeit," in *Shakespeares Stil: Germanisches und romanisches Vokabular* (Frankfurt/Main, 1973), ch. I.
5. Starnes-Noyes★
6. Nagashima★, ch. IV.
7. Noland, Daniel Woodring, "John Minsheu's *Ductor in Linguas* and the Beginning of English Historical Lexicography" (Ph. D. Dissertation, University of Texas at Austin, 1987).
8. Rosier, James L., "The Sources and Methods of Minsheu's *Guide into the Tongues,*" *Philological Quarterly,* 40 (1961), 68–76.
9. Schäfer, Jürgen, "John Minsheu: Scholar or Charlatan?," *Renaissance Quarterly,* 26 (1973), 23–35.
10. Skeat, Walter W., *Principles of English Etymology,* Second Series: *The Foreign Element* (Oxford, 1891), ch. XXV.

56. Kemble, Thorpe and Bosworth

1. Wiley, Raymond A., "Anglo-Saxon Kemble: The Life and Works of John Mitchell Kemble 1807–1857, Philologist, Historian, Archaeologist," in *Anglo-Saxon Studies in Archaeology and History I,* ed. Sonia Chadwick Hawkes, David Brown and James Campbell, BAR, British Series, 72 (Oxford, 1979), pp. 165–273. See also J. N. L. Myres, *The English Settlements,* corr. ed. (Oxford, 1989), pp. 232–33.

2. *John Mitchell Kemble and Jacob Grimm: A Correspondence 1832–1852,* ed. and trans. Raymond A. Wiley (Leiden, 1971).
3. Westphalen, Tilman, *Beowulf 3150–55: Textkritik und Editionsgeschichte,* Bochumer Arbeiten zur Sprach- und Literaturwissenschaft, 2 (Munich, 1967), esp. ch. I.4. [About Benjamin Thorpe]
4. Stanley, E. G., "J. Bosworth's Interest in 'Friesic' for his Dictionary of the Anglo-Saxon Language," in *Aspects of Old Frisian Philology,* ed. Rolf H. Bremmer, Geart van der Meer and Oebele Vries, Amsterdamer Beiträge zur älteren Germanistik, 31–32 (Amsterdam, 1990), pp. 428–52.

57. Historical linguistics in England and North America in the 19th century
— see also section 59 and note 41 on p. 63 —

1. Kennedy★, 353–506, 541–635, 2392–423, 12984–3048.
2. Aarsleff (1967)★
3. Beyer★
4. Jankowsky, Kurt R., "F. Max Müller and the Development of Linguistic Science," *HL,* 6 (1979), 339–59.
5. Mitchell, T. F., "Linguistics and Linguists in Victorian England," *ZAA,* 25 (1977), 133–47.
6. Palmer, D. J., *The Rise of English Studies: An Account of the Study of English Language and Literature from its Origins to the Making of the Oxford English School* (London, 1965).
7. Alston, R. C., "English Studies," in *The New Cambridge Bibliography of English Literature,* ed. George Watson *et al.,* 5 vols (Cambridge, 1969–1977), vol. III (1969), 1635–68.
8. Franklin, Phyllis, "English Studies: The World of Scholarship in 1883," *PMLA,* 99 (1984), 356–70.
9. Read, Allen Walker, "The Spread of German Linguistic Learning in New England during the Lifetime of Noah Webster," *American Speech,* 41 (1966), 163–81.
10. Thompson, C. R., "The Study of Anglo-Saxon in America," *ES,* 18 (1936), 241–53.

58. *The Oxford English Dictionary*

1. Kennedy*, 713–66.
2. Bivens, Leslie, "Nineteenth Century Reactions to the *O. E. D.*: An Annotated Bibliography," *Dictionaries*, 3 (1980/1981), 146–52.
3. *The Oxford English Dictionary*, ed. James A. H. Murray, Henry Bradley, W. A. Craigie and C. T. Onions, corr. re-issue, vol. I (Oxford, 1933), vii–xxvi ("Historical Introduction") and v–vi ("Preface"). See also "The History of the Oxford English Dictionary," in *The Oxford English Dictionary*, sec. ed., prepared by J. A. Simpson and E. S. C. Weiner, vol. I (Oxford, 1989), xxxv–lxi.
4. Burchfield, R. W., "Prefaces" to the four supplementary volumes to *The Oxford English Dictionary* (Oxford, 1972–1986).
5. Aarsleff (1967)*, ch. VI.
6. Benzie, William, *Dr. F. J. Furnivall: Victorian Scholar Adventurer* (Norman, Oklahoma, 1983).
7. Murray, K. M. Elisabeth, *Caught in the Web of Words: James A. H. Murray and the Oxford English Dictionary* (New Haven, 1977).
8. Schäfer, Jürgen, *Documentation in the O. E. D.: Shakespeare and Nashe as Test Cases* (Oxford, 1980).

59. English as an academic discipline

1. Aarsleff (1967)*
2. Chambers, R. W., *Man's Unconquerable Mind: Studies of English Writers, from Bede to A. E. Housman and W. P. Ker* (London, 1939), ch. XI.
3. Christmann, Hans Helmut, *Romanistik und Anglistik an den deutschen Universitäten im 19. Jahrhundert: Ihre Herausbildung als Fächer und ihr Verhältnis zu Germanistik und Klassischer Philologie* (Stuttgart, 1985).
4. Finkenstaedt, Thomas and Gertrud Scholtes, eds, *Towards a History of English Studies in Europe: Proceedings of the Wildsteig-Symposium, April 30–May 3, 1982*, Augsburger I&I-Schriften, 21 (Augsburg, 1983).
5. Finkenstaedt, Thomas, *Kleine Geschichte der Anglistik in Deutschland: Eine Einführung* (Darmstadt, 1983).
6. Franklin (1984) [cf. 57.8.]
7. Haenicke, Gunta, *Zur Geschichte der Anglistik an deutschsprachigen Universitäten 1850–1925*, Augsburger I&I-Schriften, 8 (Augsburg, 1979).
8. Haenicke and Finkenstaedt (1992) [cf. 6.5.]

9. McMurtry, Jo, *English Language, English Literature: The Creation of an Academic Discipline* (Hamden, Conn., 1985).
10. Palmer (1965) [cf. 57.6.]

60. English grammar since the late 19th century

1. Kennedy*, 6086–156.
2. Aarts, Flor, "English Grammars and the Dutch Contribution: 1891–1985," in Leitner (1986)*, pp. 363–86.
3. Funke, Otto, "On the System of Grammar," *Archivum Linguisticum*, 6 (1954), 1–19.
4. Leitner (1986) [cf. 47.3.]
5. Leitner, Gerhard, "English Grammars—Past, Present and Future," in Leitner (1986)*, pp. 409–31.
6. Leitner, Gerhard, "English Grammaticology," *International Review of Applied Linguistics in Language Teaching*, 23 (1985), 199–215.
7. Leitner (1991)*
8. McKay, John C., *A Guide to Germanic Reference Grammars: The Modern Standard Languages,* Amsterdam Studies in the Theory and History of Linguistic Science V, 15 (Amsterdam, 1984), pp. 93–129.
9. Welte (1985) [cf. 5.9.], pp. 91–8. [On Jespersen's grammatical system]
10. Zandvoort, Reinerd W., "Three Grammarians: Poutsma - Jespersen - Kruisinga," *Moderna Språk,* 52 (1958), 2–14 [= R. W. Zandvoort, *Collected Papers II: Articles in English Published between 1955 and 1970,* Groningen Studies in English, 10 (Groningen, 1970), pp. 85–96].
11. Jespersen, Otto, "The System of Grammar," in *Linguistica: Selected Papers in English, French and German* (Copenhagen, 1933), pp. 304–45.
12. Funke, Otto, "Jespersens Lehre von den 'Three Ranks'," *Englische Studien,* 60 (1925/1926), 140–57.
13. Walmsley, John, "The Sonnenschein v. Jespersen Controversy," in *Meaning and Beyond: Ernst Leisi zum 70. Geburtstag,* ed. Udo Fries and Martin Heusser (Tübingen, 1989), pp. 253–81.
14. Walmsley, John, "E. A. Sonnenschein and Grammatical Terminology," in Leitner (1991)*, pp. 57–80.

61. Usage
— see also section 38 —

1. Kennedy*, 5499–686, 12577–97.
2. Baron (1982) [cf. 32.6.]

3. Burchfield, Robert, "The Fowler Brothers and the Tradition of Usage Handbooks," in Leitner (1991)*, pp. 93–111.

4. Finegan, Edward, *Attitudes toward English Usage. The History of a War of Words* (New York, 1980).

5. McKnight*, ch. XX.

6. Mencken-McDavid*, ch. IX.1.

7. Meseck, Birgit, *Studien zur konservativ-restaurativen Sprachkritik in Amerika,* Bamberger Beiträge zur englischen Sprachwissenschaft, 20 (Frankfurt/Main, 1987).

8. Pyles, Thomas, *Selected Essays on English Usage,* ed. John Algeo (Gainesville, Florida, 1979), esp. chs 19–21.

9. Smith, James W., "A Sketch of the History of the Dictionary of English Usage," in *Papers on Lexicography in Honor of Warren N. Cordell,* ed. J. E. Congleton, J. Edward Gates and Donald Hobar (Terre Haute, Ind., 1979), pp. 47–58.

10. Storm (1892) [cf. 62.7.], pp. 699–766.

11. Wells (1973) [cf. 42.30.], ch. 5.

62. History of English phonetics
— see also section 32 —

1. Austerlitz, Robert, "Historiography of Phonetics: A Bibliography," in Sebeok (1975)*, 1179–1209.

2. Kennedy*, 772–1018, 13329–32a.

3. Bronstein, Arthur J., Lawrence J. Raphael and C. J. Stevens, eds, *A Biographical Dictionary of the Phonetic Sciences* (New York, 1977).

4. Essen, Otto v., *Allgemeine und angewandte Phonetik,* fifth ed. (Berlin, 1979), ch. I.2.

5. Gimson, A. C., *An Introduction to the Pronunciation of English,* fourth ed. (London, 1989), ch. 6.

6. Jespersen, Otto, "Zur Geschichte der älteren Phonetik," in *Linguistica: Selected Papers in English, French and German* (Copenhagen, 1933), pp. 40–80. [Originally published in Danish, 1897]

7. Storm, Johan, *Englische Philologie: Anleitung zum wissenschaftlichen Studium der englischen Sprache,* sec. ed., vol. I: *Die lebende Sprache, 1. Abteilung: Phonetik und Aussprache* (Leipzig, 1892).

8. Abercrombie (1965) [cf. 33.3.]

9. Asher, R. E. and Eugénie J. A. Henderson, eds, *Towards a History of Phonetics* (Edinburgh, 1981).

10. Dobson (1968) [cf. 32.3.]

11. Firth, J. R., "The English School of Phonetics," in *Papers in Linguistics 1934–1951* (London, 1957), pp. 92–120. [Originally in *TPS* (1946), 92–132.]

12. Gimson, A. C., "Daniel Jones and Standards of English Pronunciation," *ES,* 58 (1977), 151–8.

13. Wallis, ed. Kemp (1972) [cf. 35.1.], "Introduction," ch. 7.

14. Lehnert, Martin, "Die Anfänge der wissenschaftlichen und praktischen Phonetik in England," *Archiv,* 173 (1938), 163–80, and 174 (1938), 28–35.

15. Percival, W. Keith, "On the Extent of Phonetic Knowledge in the Middle Ages," in Asbach-Schnitker and Roggenhofer (1987) [cf. 40.8.], pp. 271–86.

16. Raudnitzky, Hans, *Die Bell-Sweetsche Schule: Ein Beitrag zur Geschichte der englischen Phonetik,* Marburger Studien zur englischen Philologie, 13 (Marburg, 1911).

17. Subbiondo, Joseph L., "John Wilkins' Theory of Articulatory Phonetics," in Aarsleff *et al.* (1987)★, pp. 263–70.

18. *The Indispensable Foundation: A Selection from the Writings of Henry Sweet,* ed. Eugénie J. A. Henderson (London, 1971).

19. Panconcelli-Calzia, Giulio, *Geschichtszahlen der Phonetik. Quellenatlas der Phonetik.* New edition with an English introduction by Konrad Koerner, SHLS, 16 (Amsterdam, 1994).

63. History of semantics

1. Kennedy★, 1803–27.

2. Collin, Carl S. R., *A Bibliographical Guide to Sematology: A List of the Most Important Works and Reviews on Sematological Subjects hitherto Published* (Lund, 1914).

3. Antal, Lazlo, ed., *Aspekte der Semantik: Zu ihrer Theorie und Geschichte, 1662–1970,* trans. Veronika Elroich and Cosima Kuci-Venegas (Frankfurt/Main, 1972).

4. Gordon, W. Terrence, *A History of Semantics,* SHLS, 30 (Amsterdam, 1982).

5. Hassler, Gerda, *Der semantische Wertbegriff in Sprachtheorien vom 18. bis zum 20. Jahrhundert* (Berlin, 1991).

6. Kronasser, Heinz, *Handbuch der Semasiologie: Kurze Einführung in die Geschichte, Problematik und Terminologie der Bedeutungslehre,* Bibliothek

der allgemeinen Sprachwissenschaft, Erste Reihe (Heidelberg, 1952), pp. 18–20 and chs 1–6.

7. Land, Stephen K., *From Signs to Propositions: The Concept of Form in Eighteenth-Century Semantic Theory,* Longman Linguistics Library, 16 (London, 1974).

8. Nerlich, Brigitte, *Semantic Theories in Europe 1830–1930: From Etymology to Contextuality,* SHLS, 59 (Amsterdam, 1992).

9. Salmon, Vivian, "Some Views on Meaning in Sixteenth-Century England," in Schmitter (1990) [cf. 46.9.], pp. 33–53.

10. Ullmann, Stephen, *Semantics: An Introduction to the Science of Meaning* (Oxford, 1962), "Introductory" and p. 196.

11. Dolezal, Fredric T., "John Wilkins and the Development of a Structural Semantics," in Aarsleff *et al.* (1987)★, pp. 271–81.

64. The study of English dialects

1. Kennedy★, 1873–995, 10623–11328, 13395–9.
2. Alston★, vol. IX (1971).
3. Wakelin, Martyn F., *English Dialects: An Introduction,* rev. ed. (London, 1977), esp. ch. 3.
4. Dieth, Eugen, "A New Survey of English Dialects," *Essays and Studies,* 32 (1947), 74–104.
5. Dietz, Klaus, "Karl Luick and Historical English Dialectology," in *Luick Revisited: Papers Read at the Luick-Symposium at Schloss Liechtenstein, 15.–18.9.1985,* ed. Dieter Kastovsky and Gero Bauer, TüBL, 288 (Tübingen, 1988), pp. 31–78.
6. Kökeritz, Helge, "Alexander Gill (1621) on the Dialects of South and East England," *Studia Neophilologica,* 11 (1938/1939), 277–88.
7. McIntosh, Angus, M. L. Samuels and Michael Benskin, *A Linguistic Atlas of Late Mediaeval English,* 4 vols (Aberdeen, 1986), I, 3–4.
8. Viereck, Wolfgang, "Englische Dialektologie," in *Germanische Dialektologie: Festschrift für Walther Mitzka zum 80. Geburtstag,* 2 vols, ed. Ludwig Erich Schmitt (Wiesbaden, 1968) [= *Zeitschrift für Mundartforschung,* Beihefte, N. F., 5–6], pp. 542–64.

65. The study of place-names and personal names

1. Kennedy★, 1420–632, 3965–4051, 5154–80, 8849–9507, 13381–92.
2. Alston★, vol. XI (1977).

3. Roberts, Richard Julian, *Bibliography of Writings on English Place- and Personal Names* (Louvain, 1961) [= *Onoma*, 8 (1958/1959), no. 3].
4. Mawer, Allen, "English Place-Name Study: Its Present Condition and Future Possibilities," *Proceedings of the British Academy*, 10 (1921–1923), 31–44.
5. Dickins, Bruce, "The Progress of English Place-Name Studies since 1901," *Antiquity*, 35 (1961), 281–5.
6. Spittal, Jeffrey and John Field, eds, *A Reader's Guide to the Place-Names of the United Kingdom. A Bibliography of Publications (1920–89) on the Place-Names of Great Britain and Northern Ireland, The Isle of Man, and The Channel Islands* (Stamford, 1990).
7. Voitl, Herbert, "Die englische Personennamenkunde: Ein Forschungsbericht," *Archiv*, 199 (1963), 158–67, and 200 (1964), 108–18, 436–50.

See 69.15. for American place-names.

66. English as a world language

1. Kennedy*, 2997–3039, 8850.
2. Bailey (1991) [cf. 5.3.]
3. [Wolfgang Viereck, Sebastian Köppl, Josef Schmied and Edgar Schneider, eds.] *Englisch: Formen und Funktionen einer Weltsprache: Ausstellung des Lehrstuhls für Englische Sprachwissenschaft und Mediävistik und der Universitätsbibliothek* (Bamberg, 1983).
4. Mencken-McDavid*, ch. XII.
5. Sonderegger, Stefan, "Jacob Grimms allgemeine Einstufung und Wertschätzung der englischen Sprache," in *The History and the Dialects of English: Festschrift for Eduard Kolb,* ed. Andreas Fischer, Anglistische Forschungen, 203 (Heidelberg, 1989), pp. 15–31.
6. Watts, T., "On the Probable Future Position of the English Language," *Proceedings of the Philological Society*, 4 (1848–1850), 207–14.

67. English in Empire and Commonwealth; Pidgins and Creoles

1. Kennedy*, 11329–56, 11782–867a.
2. *Englisch: Formen und Funktionen* (1983) [cf. 66.3.]
3. Spies, Heinrich, *Kultur und Sprache im neuen England*, sec. ed. (Leipzig, 1928).

4. Avis, Walter S. and A. M. Kinloch, *Writings on Canadian English 1792–1975: An Annotated Bibliography* (Toronto, 1978).

5. Goetsch, Paul, "Das kanadische Englisch: Ein Forschungsbericht," *Anglia,* 81 (1963), 56–81.

6. Avis, Walter S., "The English Language in Canada," in *Current Trends in Linguistics,* ed. Thomas A. Sebeok *et al.,* 14 vols in 21 (The Hague, 1963–1976), vol. X: *Linguistics in North America,* in 2 vols (1973), 40–74.

7. Turner, G. W., *The English Language in Australia and New Zealand* (London, 1966), ch. 2.

8. Ramson, W. S., "Nineteenth-Century Australian English," in *English Transported: Essays on Australasian English,* ed. W. S. Ramson (Canberra, 1970), pp. 32–48.

9. Hellinger, Marlis, *Englisch-orientierte Pidgin- und Kreolsprachen: Entstehung, Geschichte und sprachlicher Wandel,* Erträge der Forschung, 221 (Darmstadt, 1985), chs 1–4.

10. Valdmann, Albert, ed., *Pidgin and Creole Linguistics* (Bloomington, Ind., 1977).

11. Fought, John, "The Reinvention of Hugo Schuchardt (Review article)," *Language in Society,* 11 (1982), 419–36.

68. Noah Webster
— see also section 69a —

1. Skeel, Emily Ellsworth Ford, *A Bibliography of the Writings of Noah Webster,* ed. Edwin H. Carpenter, Jr (New York, 1958).

2. Ford, Emily Ellsworth Fowler, *Notes on the Life of Noah Webster,* ed. Emily Ellsworth Ford Skeel, 2 vols (New York, privately printed, 1912).

3. Malone, Kemp, "A Linguistic Patriot," *American Speech,* 1 (1925), 26–31.

4. Pyles, Thomas, *Words and Ways of American English* (New York, 1952), ch. 5.

5. Reed, Joseph W., Jr, "Noah Webster's Debt to Samuel Johnson," *American Speech,* 37 (1962), 95–105.

6. Southard, Bruce, "Noah Webster: America's Forgotten Linguist," *American Speech,* 54 (1979), 12–22.

7. Warfel, Harry R., *Noah Webster: Schoolmaster to America* (New York, 1936).

8. Wells (1973) [cf. 42.30.], ch. 3.

69. American English

1. Kennedy★, 11357–780, 9508–615.
2. Brenni, Vito J., *American English: A Bibliography* (Philadelphia, 1964).
3. Baugh-Cable★, ch. 11.
4. Galinsky, Hans, *Das amerikanische Englisch: Seine innere Entwicklung und internationale Ausstrahlung. Ein kritischer Forschungsbericht als Einführung in die Grundlegungsphase der sprachwissenschaftlichen Amerikanistik (1919–1945)*, Erträge der Forschung, 125 (Darmstadt, 1979).
5. Laird, Charlton, *Language in America* (New York, 1970).
6. McDavid, Raven I., Jr, "The English Language in the United States," in Sebeok, vol. X (1973) [cf. 67.6.], 10–39.
7. McDavid, Raven I., Jr, "American English: A Bibliographic Essay," *American Studies International,* 17,2 (1979), 3–45.
8. Mencken-McDavid★, chs I,1.–8.
9. Mathews, M. M., *The Beginnings of American English: Essays and Comments* (Chicago, 1931).
10. Meseck (1987) [cf. 61.7.]
11. Mesick, Jane Louise, *The English Traveller in America 1785–1835,* Columbia University Studies in English and Comparative Literature, 23 (New York, 1922).
12. Simpson, David, *The Politics of American English, 1776–1850* (New York, 1986).
13. Atwood, E. Bagby, "Amerikanische Dialektologie," trans. Frank Schindler, in L. E. Schmitt (1968) [cf. 64.8.], pp. 565–600.
14. Burke (1939) [cf. 42b.3.]
15. Sealock, Richard B., Margaret M. Sealock and Margaret S. Powell, *Bibliography of Place-Name Literature: United States and Canada,* third ed. (Chicago, 1982).

69a. American lexicography
— see also section 42 —

1. Algeo, John, "American Lexicography," in *WDD*★, vol. II, sect. 200.
2. Burkett, Eva Mae, *American Dictionaries of the English Language before 1861* (Metuchen, N. J., 1979). [Based on the author's 1936 Dissertation; not updated]

3. Friend, Joseph H., *The Development of American Lexicography 1798–1864*, JL, Series Practica, 37 (The Hague, 1967).
4. Krapp, George Philip, *The English Language in America*, 2 vols (New York, 1925), vol. I, ch. VII.

70. Linguistics in the 20th century: some comprehensive treatments

1. Reichl (1993) [cf. 1.7.], sect. II. B.
2. Sebeok (1975)★
3. Arens (1969)★, part 3.
4. Robins (1990)★, ch. 8.
5. Albrecht, Jörn, *Europäischer Strukturalismus: Ein forschungsgeschichtlicher Überblick* (Darmstadt, 1988).
6. Bolton, W. F. and D. Crystal, eds, *The English Language*, 2 vols (Cambridge, 1966–1969), vol. II (1969): *Essays by Linguists and Men of Letters: 1858–1964*.
7. Christmann, Hans Helmut, *Idealistische Philologie und moderne Sprachwissenschaft*, Internationale Bibliothek für Allgemeine Linguistik, 19 (Munich, 1974).
8. Coseriu, Eugenio, *Einführung in die strukturelle Linguistik* (Tübingen, 1969).
9. Davis, Philip W., *Modern Theories of Language* (Englewood Cliffs, N. J., 1973).
10. *A Geneva School Reader in Linguistics*, ed. Robert A. Godel (Bloomington, Ind., 1969).
11. Harris, Roy, ed., *Linguistic Thought in England 1914–1945* (London, 1988).
12. Helbig, Gerhard, *Geschichte der neueren Sprachwissenschaft: Unter dem besonderen Aspekt der Grammatik-Theorie* (Leipzig, 1970).
13. Helbig, Gerhard, *Die Entwicklung der Sprachwissenschaft seit 1970* (Leipzig, 1986).
14. Herndon, Jeanne H., *A Survey of Modern Grammars*, sec. ed. (New York, 1976).
15. Ivić (1965) [cf. 4.10.], chs 13–18.
16. Langendoen, D. Terence, *The London School of Linguistics: A Study of the Linguistic Theories of B. Malinowski and J. R. Firth*, Research Monograph, 46 (Cambridge, Mass., 1968).
17. Lehmann, Winfred P., *Linguistische Theorien der Moderne*, Germanistische Lehrbuchsammlung, 19a (Berne, 1981).

18. Lepschy, Guilio C., *A Survey of Structural Linguistics,* sec. ed. (London, 1982).
19. Leroy, Maurice, *Les grands courants de la linguistique moderne,* sec. ed., Université Libre de Bruxelles, Travaux de la Faculté de Philosophie et Lettres, 24 (Brussels, 1963). [English translation by Glanville Price, *The Main Trends in Modern Linguistics* (Oxford, 1967).]
20. Malmberg, Bertil, *New Trends in Linguistics: An Orientation,* trans. Edward Carney, Bibliotheca Linguistica, Guides to Modern Theories and Methods, 1 (Stockholm, 1964). [Original ed. in Swedish, 1959]
21. Mohrmann, Christine, Alf Sommerfelt and Joshua Whatmough, eds, *Trends in European and American Linguistics 1930–1960* (Utrecht, 1961).
22. Newmeyer, Frederick J., *Linguistic Theory in America. The First Quarter-Century of Transformational Generative Grammar,* sec. ed. (New York, 1986).
23. Robins (1973) [cf. 4.13.]
24. Sampson, Geoffrey, *Schools of Linguistics: Competition and Evolution* (London, 1980).
25. Szemerényi, Oswald, *Richtungen der modernen Sprachwissenschaft,* 2 vols (Heidelberg, 1971–1982).
26. *A Prague School Reader in Linguistics,* compil. Josef Vachek, Indiana University Studies in the History and Theory of Linguistics (Bloomington, Ind., 1964).
27. Vachek, Josef, *The Linguistic School of Prague: An Introduction to its Theory and Practice* (Bloomington, Ind., 1966).

71. Some linguists of the late 19th and 20th centuries
— see also section 6 and note 41 on p. 63 —

1. Holdcroft, David, *Saussure: Signs, System and Arbitrariness* (Cambridge, 1991).
2. Koerner, E. F. K., *Ferdinand de Saussure: Origin and Development of his Linguistic Thought in Western Studies of Language: A Contribution to the History and Theory of Linguistics,* Schriften zur Linguistik, 7 (Braunschweig, 1973).
3. Juul, Arne and Hans F. Nielsen, eds, *Otto Jespersen: Facets of his Life and Work,* SHLS, 52 (Amsterdam, 1989).
4. Koerner, Konrad, ed., *Edward Sapir: Appraisals of his Life and Work,* SHLS, 36 (Amsterdam, 1984).
5. Hall, Robert A. and Konrad Koerner, eds, *Leonard Bloomfield. Essays on his Life and Work,* SHLS, 47 (Amsterdam, 1987).

6. Pocklington, Jackie, *Charles Carpenter Fries the Humanist, the Linguist, the Teacher. A Comparison with Leonard Bloomfield* (Wilhelmsfeld, 1990).
7. *First Person Singular. Papers from the Conference on an Oral Archive for the History of American Linguistics (Charlotte, N. C., 9–10 March 1979),* ed. Boyd H. Davis and Raymond K. O'Cain, SHLS, 21 (Amsterdam, 1980).
8. *First Person Singular II. Autobiographies by North American Scholars in the Language Sciences,* ed. Konrad Koerner, SHLS, 61 (Amsterdam, 1991).

Index to Part I

Personal names in Part I (pp. 1–70). References are to pages.

Index to Part II

Authors and editors of publications recorded in the Bibliography (Part II) and in the footnotes to Part I.

References prefixed 'F' are to the footnotes in Part I. 'AT' refers to the list of abbreviations and abbreviated titles on pp. 72–75. All other references give the numbers of section and item in the Bibliography. Full Christian names instead of initials in the publications have been supplied as far as possible.

⏃RTS

⏃EDIEVAL & RENAISSANCE TEXTS & STUDIES
is the publishing program of the
Center for Medieval and Early Renaissance Studies
at the State University of New York at Binghamton.

⏃RTS emphasizes books that are needed —
texts, translations, and major research tools.

⏃RTS aims to publish the highest quality scholarship
in attractive and durable format at modest cost.